Leith-Built Ships, Vol. IV

LEITH-BUILT SHIPS

VOLUME 4

ROBB CALEDON (LEITH DIVISION) (1965–1984)

R O NEISH

Whittles Publishing

Published by
Whittles Publishing Ltd,
Dunbeath,
Caithness, KW6 6EG,
Scotland, UK
www.whittlespublishing.com

By the same author:

Leith-Built Ships Volume I
They Once Were Shipbuilders
ISBN 978-184995-443-3

Leith-Built Ships Volume II
Leith Shipyards 1918-1939
ISBN 978-184995-481-5

Leith-Built Ships Volume III
Henry Robb Ltd. (1945-1965)
ISBN 978-184995-507-2

Bustler Class Rescue Tugs
In War and Peace
ISBN 978-184995-504-1

Printed and bound in Great Britain by
TJ Books Limited, Padstow, Cornwall

CONTENTS

ACKNOWLEDGEMENTS

This series of books would not have been possible without the help of many people, some sadly no longer with us. If I have missed anyone out, this is only down to my own forgetfulness, and I apologise in advance; you know who you are, and you have my thanks.

To the loftsmen at the Henry Robb shipyard, who all helped to instil a sense of pride in ships and in the craft. I must also thank Robert Rowbottom once more, as you helped me more than you could have envisaged.

To all the men of the Leith Shipyard who influenced me in one way or another.

I have tried where I can to credit all photographs and/or stories used; if a credit is missed and you contact me through the publishers, then this can be corrected in the next print run.

To Bob Sickles, ex-publisher of upstate New York, who encouraged me to pick up my writing again after I had all but given it up.

It would be remiss of me not to mention the ex-Robbs engineer J. Stevenson, who provided me with some initial information; B. Booth, shipwright, for many photographs; and the archivists at Glasgow University for allowing me access to the wonderful Leith, Hull & Hamburg/Currie Line archive.

To K. Scovell for your insight into the Currie Line.

To the Scottish Records office for some initial help with information.

To Dr Stephen Gapps and your team at the Australian Maritime Museum.

To Dr William Collier and archivist Kathryn Preston from the oldest ship design house in the world, G.L. Watson Ltd, now back where they began in Glasgow, who provided help, encouragement and some wonderful old original photographs.

To Lindsay Butterfield and all the other guys in New Zealand and Australia, who provided help and information – *way* too many people to list here!

To the many contributors to my website on the Leith Shipyards – it would be impossible to mention everyone – thanks to all.

To my editor Anne Hamilton of WriteRight Editing Services at http://www. writerightediting.co.uk, who took the job on and helped me immensely in the editing/layout parts of my book before sending it to the publishers.

To Dr Keith Whittles and his team for believing in my project, and allowing me to bring this series of books to a wider public.

To Caroline Petherick at https://www.the-wordsmith.co.uk, for providing great direction and guidance in the completion of my book; she has been a pleasure to work with, while helping with some pretty complex and technical-type details throughout this book.

To my darling wife Angie, who has the patience of a saint, always believing in me and encouraging me to reach for my dreams, to never give up, and always to persevere.

The mighty *S A Wolraad Woltemade*, Ship No 516 (image from own collection).

PREFACE

On an August morning in 1971 I wandered into the Robb Caledon yard at the Victoria shipyards. Although I was a callow 16-year-old, I did not know nothing at all, having spent a full year at technical college after leaving school at 15 (the legal leaving age in those days). As a local Leith boy, I would naturally find my way into something to do with ships or the sea. I was fascinated by the size of the place, the red-painted lumps of steel lying all over the place, and the deafening noise of a real working shipyard.

There seemed to be ships all around the place, with workers swarming all over them. I remember that the Antarctic survey ship *Bransfield* was being fitted out at the quayside, and the huge tug *Lloydsman* was on the building berth, just a month from being launched.

For me, then, it was to be another year of learning, this time in the shipyard training school, where they were to teach us all about building ships. (Yeah, right ...) From there the star apprentices were picked to serve the rest of their apprenticeship in the shipyard loft, to learn the black art of the loftsman.

The loftsmen – and I became one of them – were the guys responsible for taking a set of naval architect's scantling lines and turning them into the finished and faired ship's lines, along with a body plan and offsets, from which the full-size body plan was drawn, down on the floor, so that the platers could bend the frames of the ship correctly. We were also to develop the hull and superstructure. In order for the plates to be formed we made templates for almost every bit of steel that made up a ship, so we were involved in the whole build process from start to finish.

I considered myself fortunate to be trained up by some of the best craftsmen in the shipyard. There were only five of them at the time, so it was a pretty specialised job. There were two shipwrights there as well, to help with the outside dimensional control work.

It always seemed to be either very busy or very quiet; this was due to the way that orders came into the yard. The loft was always first to work on any order, and we would follow it all the way through – even to putting the load lines and draught marks on the vessel. Over the course of the build, we loftsmen would get to know every single frame line on a ship, and we also developed every single plate so that it could be made up correctly.

It really was the most interesting job, and I learnt things then that were to go with me into other industries and benefit me. To quote a comment on the Leith-built Ships blog, http://leithbuiltships.blogspot.com, it was a start to a working life just not possible in today's world.

During my apprenticeship there were a couple of ro/ro container ships being built. Then while I was working as a loftsman Robbs also got an order to build three ships for the Admiralty, at least two of which would serve in the Falklands conflict – one of them, HMS *Herald*, converted into a hospital ship, and one as a heavy lift supply/safety ship.

Working in a shipyard was a love–hate affair for me, at least, and I'm happy to say that most of the time I loved it. So many characters worked there, and I know a lot of them are still around, so I shall refrain from mentioning names. The fact that the very funny Billy Connolly was an ex-shipyard welder meant that he had no shortage of material. I will say too that, it being the 1970s and into the 1980s, there were some funny hair styles for sure.

On reflection it was a funny place as a whole, with all the different trades and factions that operated in the yard, and then there were the management, who were on the whole okay. except for the higher-up ones at yard/director level, who used to treat people as if they were something unwelcome that they had found on their shoe. They were not local. They would have been better being around in Victorian times (it wouldn't have made them any better humans, just more suited to the times). That is all I shall say about them.

I dare say that they felt the same way about the men – and remember this was in a time when personnel management was unheard of, and health & safety was a notice on a wall some place that no one looked at.

The only people supplied with a hard hat were three or four of the above-mentioned manager types. In those days the yard was a dangerous place to work in, and I even remember the so-called medical centre was in fact a small cubicle based inside the gents' toilet – no joke. The medical guy's name was Joe, and he used to double up as the toilet cleaner – management making sure he had enough work to justify him being there. If you had anything that required more than an aspirin or a plaster, then it was off with you to the local hospital in Leith.

There were the inevitable strikes, of course, as the yard was a closed shop and we were always trying to get better pay and conditions. The place had never progressed since wartime, and in fact a lot of the machinery the guys had to work on was from the previous century. I kid you not, there were rolling machines and bending machines stamped with dates from the late 19th century – and this was at a time when the industry was struggling to survive in a world market and wondering why the Japanese and others were streets ahead when it came to delivery times and costs.

While Robbs was building HMS *Herald*, HMS *Goosander* and HMS *Pochard*, while striving to win more orders to keep the place going, the next on the stocks was an order for Caledonian MacBrayne, for a passenger/car ferry to be called *Pioneer*.

Then came Ship No 516, the largest and most powerful ocean-going salvage tug in the world at the time, *S A Wolraad Woltemade*. She was one of my favourite ships.

There is an immense sense of pride felt when the ship that you have helped to build slips

HMS *Herald*, Ship No 512, on the stocks.

down the ways and into the water for the first time – a pride in accomplishment that is in my opinion unequalled in any other industry.

At the same time, three tugs were to be built that would ply their trade in the River Forth for a while, looking after tankers coming to offload crude at the Hound Point terminal – which, by the way, had been built in the yard as well. This was regarded as a plum job at the time, because as an apprentice working on it you got an extra 5p per hour – yes, I *did* say 5 pence: the good old days!

Robbs was then to build the largest ship ever built in the Leith yard; *Garrison Point*, at nearly 8,000 tonnes the longest and biggest.

This was a busy time for the yard and lots of employment for a short while, but there was always the worry of there not being another order just around the corner, and of course the management played upon this to get their way.

The gas tanker *Borthwick* was built at that time, and another ferry for CalMac, but we were now into the Thatcher era, with the threat of no work always on the horizon.

Robbs got allocated a couple of crane barges from a huge Polish order secured by the government at the time; most other yards got a bigger share, but as Robbs was in a staunch Labour ward the Tories had no chance of getting back in there, so I reckon the policy was just to give the yard bits of the large order and send the majority of the order to yards that were in marginal seats. It all boils down to politics, and that business is probably just as dirty as shipbuilding. In fact the only time any money was ever spent on cleaning up the yard was when some personage was to visit for a look around.

The early 1980s was a time of huge unrest amongst the workers in the UK, and the yard would be full of rumour and counter-rumour. I left the place for a little while, then was asked back. In the meantime a couple of tugs had been built for Nigeria, and work was going on for a couple of North Sea supply ships, along with a new lighthouse tender for Trinity House.

But the yard had changed; it just did not seem to be the same place any more. A lot of the feeling of camaraderie had gone, and I think there was a new feeling of 'look after yourself'.

Much of the older craftsmanship had gone out the door, too, when many of the men took redundancy, not caring to wait until the inevitable happened, as it did two or three years later.

The place had been too slow to change, and too slow to embrace changes in working practices and technology; and it had been given too little investment (makes you wonder where all the money went in the good times). It was dying a slow death.

The small yards, as part of the nationalised British Shipbuilders, had no voice.

We won an order from Sealink for two vessels, which at the time we did not realise were to be the last vessels launched in Leith, bringing to an end over 600 years of a proud shipbuilding tradition. This was not a good time to be relying on the incumbent Tory government for work, and the inevitable was going to happen even though we tried to fight on and keep the work in Leith.

A sad end – but I am always proud of the fact that I served my apprenticeship as a loftsman in the Henry Robb shipyard, and worked with some of the best and finest craftsmen in the industry. It is something ingrained into you, and I for one will never forget where I started out.

As I have subsequently worked my way around the world in a few different industries, it has always irked me that I could find lots of information on all the other great shipbuilding centres around the British Isles but very little about shipbuilding at Leith.

So as no one appeared to be doing anything about it, I took it upon myself to bring to light some of the forgotten maritime history of the Port of Leith. Hence this series of books.

Shipyards, by their very nature and location, became part of the social fabric and psyche of the local community. As such, it is almost incomprehensible to understand how this once great industry was allowed to go from building around 81.7 per cent of all the mercantile ships in the world in 1893, to almost none less than 100 years later. I was very lucky to serve my time as a loftsman in the shipyard that was Henry Robb Limited at Leith. When I started my apprenticeship there, the loftsmen, all very skilled craftsmen, were (in no particular order) Peter Rennie, Jim Russell, Willie Weir, Ali Holland and John Conafray, along with the foreman, Bill Straun. Each of them left many positives with me, but a special mention must go to Jim Russell, retired foreman loftsman. It was Jim who supplied me with the *Shipyard Build Book*, a full list of ships built at the Henry Robb Shipyard from Ship No 1 to the last ship built, No 535. I must also mark the contributions made by Robert Rowbottom, the last naval architect to work in the Henry Robb Shipyard, who has been unstinting in his encouragement and information.

This, then, is the fourth volume in the series of the ships built at the Leith Shipyards; the story of the yard, and of some of the 1,150 ships built there. This volume covers the period from 1965 to the closure of the yard in 1984.

NB Any opinion given is entirely my own, along with any mistakes, omissions or errors. I welcome corrections to the histories, and can be contacted through the publisher.

ABBREVIATIONS

The list below expands the abbreviations used in this series, and at the end of the book you will find a glossary of shipbuilding and nautical terms.

ABV	armed boarding vessel
aux	auxiliary motor
bhp	brake horsepower
CS	cable ship
DAMS	defensively armed merchant ship
DEMS	defensively equipped merchant ship
DWT	deadweight tons
FV	fishing vessel
grt	gross registered tonnage
HMAS	His Majesty's Australian ship
HMNZT	His Majesty's New Zealand transport
HMS	His Majesty's ship
HMT	His Majesty's trawler
ihp	indicated horsepower
LBP	length between perpendiculars (see Glossary, under AP)
LOA	length overall; the maximum length of the vessel
LWL	length at waterline
MT	motor tug
M/T	measurement ton (see Glossary, under Ton)
MV	motor vessel
nhp	nominal horsepower

ON	official number
PS	paddle steamer
PSS	paddle steamship
PTB	patrol boat
RFA	royal fleet auxiliary
rhp	rated horsepower
RMS	Royal Mail ship
RNLI	Royal National Lifeboat Institute
scr	screw-propelled; the vessel has a shaft driving a propeller (as against paddle-wheel propulsion)
shp	shaft horsepower
SMS	Seiner Majestät Schiff (His Majesty's ship)
SS	Steamship/ Screw ship
ST	Steam Tug
SWPS	Stern-Wheel Paddle Steamer
SY	Steam Yacht
THV	Trinity House Vessel
TM	Thames measurement
TS	twin screw
TSM	twin-screw motor
TSMV	twin-screw motor vessel
TSMY	twin-screw motor yacht
TSS	twin-screw steamer
TSSY	twin-screw steam yacht
U-boat	*unterseeboot* (under-sea boat), identified by the letters UB, then the given number
USS	United States ship
W/T	weight ton (see Glossary, under Ton)

From *British Shipbuilding Yards* by Norman L. Middlemiss, 1995, here are some of the many and often mysteriously-named crafts and skills required to build and repair ships:

Anglesmiths, Blacksmiths, Boatbuilders, Boilermakers, Brass Finishers, Bumpers Up, Burners, Cabinet Makers, Caulkers, Chargehands, Countersinkers, Cranemen, Draughtsmen, Drillers, Electricians, Engineers, Estimators, Fettlers, Fitters, Foremen, Frame Turners, French Polishers, Furnacemen, Holders Up, Iron Saw Men, Joiners, Labourers, Loftsmen, Machinists, Managers, Millwrights, Painters, Pattern Makers, Planers, Platers, Plumbers, Redleaders, Riggers, Riveters, Sailmakers, Sawyers, Scarphers, Stagers, Sheet Metal Men, Shipwrights, Storemen, Toolsmiths, Turners, Welders, Winchmen.

The magnificent *S A Wolraad Woltemade*, Ship No 516, in dry dock at
Singapore (image from Kit Cooper, her second engineer).

VOLUME IV – THE CONTEXT

This, the last volume in this series, chronologically speaking, is the story of the shipyards from 1965 onwards – for some of those yards a time of hope and prosperity, along with a full order book. The story of the ships built during the dark days of the Second World War will be produced in a fifth book, to complete the history of the ships built at Leith.

ONE
THE S CLASS SHIPS

FOR THE WILSON & PAPAYANNI LINES

The 1960s was a reasonably good time for the shipbuilders of Leith, with a busy order book, and it was a decade that saw the yard go over completely to all-welded ships. In the winter of 1964 a sense of excitement built, as the Henry Robb Shipyard had just won its largest single order for ships since the Second World War. This order would keep the yard busy for the next three to four years.

The order had come from the Ellerman Wilson Line, and was for a total of seven ships, of which five were to form the new S class of cargo vessel for the Wilson Line of Hull, the other two to be for the Papayanni Line. The ships were to be a new design for small bulk carriers. All seven ships had the same dimensions except the final one; all had the same engine type.

All the Wilson Line ships had names ending with the letter O, part of the long tradition of the line; while the Wilson Line was a part of the huge Ellerman Group, it was still run as an independent entity, with its own long traditions and ship-naming conventions left intact.

The Papayanni Line was another of the independent lines within the Ellerman Group, and it too kept to its own long line of tradition when it came to ship names; all the Papayanni Line ships ended with the letters 'ian'.

The shipyards at Leith had built many vessels for the Ellerman Line and associated companies. This company was one of the Leith Shipyard's biggest customers.

Although the order was for more functional and less elegant ships than the previous Ellerman vessels built in the yard, it was a very welcome order, and the ships were built to the highest standards of craftsmanship.

All five of the Wilson ships were identical sisters, with the same grt at 1,559 tons, and only the final Wilson ship, the *Sangro*, with a different deck crane arrangement. The previous S class ships all had the Thomson derrick aft, just in front of the bridge, while the *Sangro* had hers placed amidships.

The Wilson Line was in the process of developing a modern fleet equipped for speedy and efficient cargo handling; the S class ships had on-board cranes to allow the handling of

Salerno was the lead ship; she was launched by Mrs Elizabeth Brown, wife of the Ellerman director Edward Brown, watched here by Henry Robb Junior.

general and containerised cargo as well as loaded pallets and refrigerated containers. They were equipped with side-loading doors, port and starboard, for driving cargo straight into the tween decks. In addition, they were fitted with bow thrusters to aid in docking – all state-of-the-art refinements for those years.

The S Class ships were fitted out to a high standard, the accommodation much appreciated by most of the crew who sailed on them. But the ships did not have the same opulence as the previous Ellerman ships built at Leith. In addition, they all had their superstructure aft, which was becoming the norm for ships at this time in a drive for increased efficiency; it created more hold space and cut down on the length of propeller shaft – a big saving for the owners.

The lead ship of this large order, *Salerno*, was to be laid down as Ship No 495 (she would not receive her official name until closer to launch day), and would always be referred by her yard number in the shipyard.

She was powered by a 6-cylinder oil engine built by Mirrlees National Ltd, Stockport, England, giving her a speed of 13 knots; her principal dimensions were length overall 308 feet with a beam of 45 feet 6 inches and a moulded depth of 26 feet. She was ready for launch in late November 1965; after outfitting and sea trials she was handed over to her owners, ready for work.

The following are some images of the launch party on the day that MV *Salerno* was launched. They sent to the author by Nick Brown, the son of Mr and Mrs Brown, and Nick is in some of the images.

Above: The assembled launch party posing for photographs before moving onto the launch platform.

Right: Mrs Brown pushes the button which rings the bell to tell the shipwrights to knock the daggers away.

Left: Some of the launch party watch *Salerno* gathering speed as she moves down the slipway into the water for another perfect launch at Leith.

Right: MV *Salerno* goes into the water with a shipwright looking on from the side of the ways.

She was the third ship of the Ellerman Line to bear the name *Salerno*, after the town of Salerno in Italy, perhaps better known as the place where, at the start of the Allied invasion of Italy during the Second World War, the main invasion force landed in Operation Avalanche, while two supporting operations took place in Calabria and Taranto.

Salerno was used on the trade routes from London to Stockholm, Gävle and Sundsvall in Sweden.

She also saw service on the Mediterranean route, with frequent stops in Lisbon. She had a couple of well-known mishaps in her time, including breaking the inner dock gates of Horten Verft, costing a couple of million Norwegian kroner, and she damaged her rudder on rocks in the Stockholm Archipelago.

As part of the Ellerman Wilson Line reorganisation around 1973/4 she was transferred into the Ellerman City Line and renamed *City of Corinth*.

She continued with the City Line for another four years before being sold on to Perivale Maritime Inc and renamed again: *Pyrgos Star*.

But *Salerno*, along with the rest of the S class, was designed, built and launched at the wrong period in history, a time when the maritime market was changing forever due to the sweeping containerisation of shipping.

Rod Baker, who was on *Salerno*, can be seen in this set of images that he sent to the author, taken while the ship was passing through the Kiel Canal in the late 1960s.

Salerno was sold by City Line in 1978 to Greek shipping interests, and after many name changes ended up registered in Ulaanbaatar, Mongolia, under her final name, *Pertama*.

Salerno had a useful working life of some 41 years. Some of her crew have memories – good and not so good – of their time aboard her:

Left: Some of *Salerno*'s crew, Christmas 1969, in Falkenstein, after the ship had collided with the Horten Verft dock gates while she was being repaired there. They were none too happy about spending Christmas away from home. Back row (L to R): Gordon McDougall – who sent the photograph to me – Mike-AB, Bert-AB. Seated (L to R) Arthur-AB and Mike Madon, cook. *Right*: *Salerno* was eventually sold for scrap, and was broken up in 2006.

Bruce LeCren:

I remember MV *Salerno* bringing the annual resupply to communities in the Canadian Arctic in the summer of 1974. I was an electronic tech at Coral Harbour, and went aboard her to repair a radio.

I remember the skipper apologising for the gift of a case of Crown Royal, saying the Canadian whiskey wasn't up to his standards. We ashore certainly felt otherwise!"

Rod Baker:

I signed on the MV *Salerno* on 14 September 1967. It was my last ship before I left for Canada. I have fond memories of the run through the Kiel Canal to Sweden, of the lovely Swedish girls that would be waiting on the dock for us when the ship arrived (Lena Johanson, where are you now?), and of making money by smuggling, booze, cigarettes, cigarette papers and chewing gum past the Swedish customs. Of very cold times spent on watch on the foc'sle head as we passed through the Kiel Canal. I got my AB's ticket on the *Salerno*, and then left the sea and England to live in Vancouver, Canada.

Gordon McDougall:

This was my first ship on leaving the training school at Gravesend. I was a catering assistant when she crashed into the inner dock gates of Horten Verft. I recall Mike Maden was the cook at that time, and following the accident we spent the Christmas and New Year in Falkenstein.

Alistair Heelas:

My dad sailed on the *Salerno*, and was taken very ill on board in 1972. He later died in the French colonial hospital in Izmir, Turkey.

Al Marjan ex-*Sorrento* at anchor after her release by pirates, in this U.S. Navy photograph.

Next on the stocks at the shipyard was the sister ship, *Salmo* (Ship No 496), launched in December 1966; she was used on the trade routes from London to the Mediterranean, with frequent stops in Malta.

As part of the Ellerman Wilson Line reorganisation around 1973/4 she was transferred into the Ellerman City Line, renamed *City of Athens*.

Sold out of the Ellerman Line in 1976, she went on to sail under various names until broken up in January 1988 at Gadani Beach. *Salmo* had a useful working life of only 20 years.

The following year saw two more of the S Class ships launched, with *Sorrento* (Ship No 497) first, in May 1967, followed by *Silvio* (Ship No 498) in November 1967; both ships were duly delivered to the Wilson Line.

Sorrento was used on the trade routes from London to Stockholm, across the unpredictable North Sea, before being sold on in the first of many such trades. First, she was transferred in 1974 to Ellerman City Line and renamed *City of Sparta*, continuing with this name for another four years.

Over the next 14 years a number of name changes followed, with her ending up as *Al Marjan*, voyaging up and down the dangerous waters of the East African coast, primarily involved in relief food efforts to the war-torn area; eventually, in October 2007, she was hijacked by Somali pirates, and was only released after payment of an undisclosed ransom. In December 2007 the US Navy dock landing ship USS *Whidbey Island* (LSD 41) was on hand to assist *Al Marjan* and her crew, following her release from the pirates.

This remarkable small cargo vessel carried on working, although under somewhat dubious circumstances. She was to meet her fate some two years after being seized by the pirates. This old S Class ship, while under the ownership of Shamir Marine, was operated by Biyat International out of the United Arab Emirates and registered in Comoros!

She caught fire while smuggling charcoal from Somalia to Oman, and burned at her mooring in Mogadishu, bringing her working life of some 43 years to a halt.

Richard Winchester:

In 1973 we took *Sorrento* across the Atlantic to sail from Montreal to the Canadian Arctic. The trip across in ballast was bad pounding all the way, then the Arctic trips dodging bergs and working cargo onto barges that were carried on deck. Then in Pond Inlet we had a blizzard that had me and Capt Needham struggling with wire ropes to try and save the barges, but we lost one; later, it was found grounded 3 miles away. We then took a cargo to Newport News followed by rolls of paper on the homeward trip to Ellesmere Port.

Silvio (Ship No 498) was the second ship built at the Leith Shipyards to bear this name, and she was the fourth ship of the Ellerman Line Group with the name. Transferred in 1974 to the City Line, she was renamed *City of Patras*. She was used on the trade routes from Hull to east Sweden and Finland most of the time, also used on the Mediterranean routes from London. She continued with the City Line for another four years before being sold on in 1978 to Ghana and renamed *City of Tema*.

She was then sold on to a number of obscure shipping lines and renamed many more times; she was last under the Cambodian flag before she was eventually broken up in July 2009. *Silvio* had a useful working life of some 42 years.

The final S class vessel for Wilson Line of Hull was *Sangro* (Ship No 499) built the same as her other four sister ships, but with, as mentioned earlier, a different deck crane arrangement.

As part of the Ellerman Wilson Line reorganisation around 1973/4 *Sangro* was transferred into the Ellerman City Line, to be renamed *City of Ankara*. Sold to Panamanian shipping interests and going through many name changes, she ended up as an Indonesian ship with the name of *Kalimantan Pacific*. While under this name she was detained at Bangkok in Thailand, before being sold and towed for demolition in Bangladesh. *Sangro* had had a useful working life of some 32 years.

The penultimate S Class vessel built at Leith, destined for use by the Papayanni Line, was *Athenian* (Ship No 501), which was launched in May 1966; with a gross tonnage of 1,589, she was almost identical to the Wilson Line ships. She was used primarily on the trade routes to the Mediterranean. As part of the Ellerman Wilson Line reorganisation around 1973/4 she was transferred into the Ellerman City Line, and renamed *City of Valletta*.

She was to stay with the Ellerman City Line until 1979, before being sold to Singapore shipping interests and renamed *Koto Jade*. She was eventually broken up in Taiwan in 1986.

This nice trim ship was to have a working life of only some 20 years.

The final ship of the seven-ship order was the second ship for the Papayanni Line; she was given

MV *Athenian*, renamed *City of Valletta*.

one of the longest names in the fleet: *Mediterranean*. How the painters of the ship in the future must have complained about repainting her name each year! She, Ship No 503, was very similar to her predecessors, but broader in the beam, which meant that her lines had to change from those of her six sister ships; she had the same engine, though, coming in at 1,459 grt. She was launched in October 1968.

She was used primarily on the trade routes to the Mediterranean; she was then transferred to Ellerman City Line, renamed *City of Istanbul*, to stay with them until 1978.

She was to have a few more names over the next 20 years, last named *Sara* in 2010, sailing under the flag of Togo and managed by shipping interests from Lebanon.

She was broken up January 2011, ending more than 44 years plying the oceans of the world.

Richard Winchester:

I was third mate on her, and whilst she was in dry dock in London she was used in *Ripping Yarns*. In some copies shown you can just make out the name.

Steve Farrar:

I sailed on her from Edinburgh to Liverpool and then on her first trip to the Mediterranean. I was the cabin boy, first time at sea.

Top left: MV *Sorrento* of the Wilson Line (part of the huge Ellerman Group).

Top right: MV *Silvio* discharging cargo with her deck cranes.

Left: Just after her launch, MV *Sangro* is being towed around to the fitting-out basin.

She was the last ship built by Robbs at Leith for the Ellerman Line, although Robbs would later build a ro-ro ferry to be managed by the line.

This was a busy time for the yard; along with a good order book, the yard was being modernised, with a reduction in the number of building berths and the construction of a new assembly hall, complete with panel line. The old berths that once formed the Cran & Somerville Shipyard were filled in, to become a steel stockyard. A couple of berths that had originally been part of the Hawthorns Shipyard were needed for the base of the new panel line.

While the S Class ships were being built, the yard was also involved in building the helicopter support ship RFA *Engadine*, Ship No 500, in September 1966.

This decade was still to produce some fine and famous ships, and work – for the first half of this ten-year period, at least – was regular. It also created lots of overtime work; compensation in a small way for the poor working conditions and relatively low pay of the shipbuilders at Leith.

TWO
RFA ENGADINE

While the build of the Ellerman Wilson ships was going on, the yard started work on the longest ship ever built in the Leith Shipyards of Henry Robb; this most welcome order had come from the Ministry of Defence.

She had been ordered by the Admiralty (MoD) in August 1964, at a time which was something of a boom for the shipyard; along with the large order for merchant ships from Ellerman Lines it was a good time to be a shipbuilder in Leith, with full employment and a large order book.

HMS *Engadine*, Ship No 500, and the second Royal Navy ship to carry the name, was to be the Royal Navy's first dedicated helicopter support ship. She was quite a vessel. She was the first purpose-built helicopter training ship in the Royal Navy, and was built to merchant ship specifications but manned by Royal Navy personnel; she had a high standard of accommodation, and was the only ship at the time in the Royal Fleet Auxiliary to be fitted with stabilisers, which had been designed by the Edinburgh firm of Brown Brothers Ltd.

Such was the workload at the yard that some of her build in modular form was sub-contracted out to a shipyard on the other side of the Forth, it was at Burtisland Shipyards on the Fife side, that some of the modules were built – nothing new here, as Henry Robb shipyards had helped to pioneer the same system to build and launch many of the ships built during the Second World War.

Indeed the two huge aircraft carriers being assembled at Rosyth on the Forth were being built the same way, through a collaboration of the small number of the shipyards that were left in the UK.

After fitting out in the basin at Leith *Engadine* was towed down the river under the Forth Railway Bridge to the then Royal Dockyard at Rosyth, to be fitted with her secret electronics.

After commission she was attached to the Western Fleet and based at Portland.

With the increasing use of helicopters from destroyers and frigates, there was a requirement to train pilots to operate in deep water, away from coastal stations. RFA *Engadine*, Britain's first purpose-built aviation support ship fulfilled this role.

Left: RFA *Engadine* leaving dry dock at Leith, bound for Rosyth.
Middle: RFA *Engadine* leaving Leith.
Right: Passing under the Forth Bridge on her way to Rosyth. (All photos Alexander Birt).

Although operated by the Royal Fleet Auxiliary, the ship was to be jointly manned by RN and RFA personnel, a small permanent RN complement augmenting the RFA personnel – an idea that was by no means popular at first. Nonetheless she would successfully train more than 100 men at a time.

In addition to four Wessex helicopters, *Engadine* could carry either two Wasps or two Sea Kings. She was also capable of operating drones. These were housed in a small hangar above her main helicopter hangar.

At the silver jubilee fleet review RFA *Engadine* carried members of the press and followed the Royal Yacht *Britannia*.

During the Falklands War she served as a helicopter repair ship under the command of Captain D.F. Freeman, where she became another of the Leith-built ships to serve in the

RFA *Engadine* was based at Portland for her entire career, though in 1976 she was deployed off Lebanon, should she be required to evacuate British nationals.

conflict with Argentina over the possession of the Falkland Islands. *Engadine* spent the entire time in San Carlos Water – Bomb Alley, as the men there called it, due to the heavy risk of attacks by the Argentine air force. *Engadine*'s role became even more important with the sinking of the container ship *Atlantic Conveyor*, which had been carrying a cargo of helicopters and spare parts plus other cargo for use in the conflict.

By the mid-1980s, RFA *Engadine* was rapidly approaching obsolescence; in 1989

RFA *Engadine* at anchor in San Carlos Water in 1982, with two Sea Kings. At the time, rumour had it that she had slipped away from home waters, and no one knew where she was until she appeared down south – it was a lovely story. (Photo taken by Mike Day, from RFA *Fort Grange*, and reproduced here with permission.)

she was laid up at Devonport. She was then sold to a private Greek company who were to continue her operating, but this came to nothing and she was laid up again until sold in 1996 for scrap; she was broken up in India, and her place was taken by RFA *Argus*, a converted merchant vessel.

The *Engadine* evoked many memories, and some are told below:

David Bolton:

I was ship's cook on the *Engadine* during the Falklands War.

Before we sailed for the operation, we had a celebration for 25,000 deck landings (more than a carrier!).

I baked a cake for it, roughly 3 feet long, and coloured and carved into a model of the ship. Captain Freeman didn't want me in the photos, but I was not leaving my cake, so got my pic taken with it.

Clive Hamilton (Taff):

I was on the ship in the Falklands as a JCR galley and steward, and I remember David Bolton and the cake … very happy times spent in the RFA, especially the *Engadine*, my first ship!!

James Morrison:

I sailed on this ship first on sea trials, when the catering was done by boys from Leith Nautical College. We were then taken on as catering boys. I stayed on the vessel for over one year. The commander of the ship was Captain Charles Stuart Bonshaw Irwin DSO DSC RD RFA. The day-to-day running was done by merchant seamen, and the Royal Navy ran the training of pilots and flight deck crew.

G.P. Connon:

I was stationed on the *Engadine* for roughly a week or 10 days during the time of her being used as a trial for Harriers.

Andrew Rennie:

The ship itself was manned by personnel of the Royal Fleet Auxiliary in a classic Merchant Navy fashion; the RN contingent purely assisted the RFA personnel in military areas, such as communications, flight deck, helicopter control, handling and operations."

For more information, go to https://historicalrfa.uk/ and search for Engadine.

THREE
FAST AND FURIOUS/
AMALGAMATION

Ships were being built as fast and as furiously as the men from Leith could go, and it's difficult to keep track of the launchings, as some ships were built out of sequence with their given numbers.

While the 1960s boom continued the management felt that it was a good time to expand the firm of Henry Robb, and it was decided that the famous old Dundee shipyard Caledon would make a good acquisition. So it was that the firm of Henry Robb effectively took over the Caledon yard. The new company was called Robb Caledon Shipbuilders Ltd, but everyone outside Caledon still called the yard at Leith by its old name, Henry Robb, or just Robbs.

The build schedule had included Ship No 502, an order from the Nigerian Port Authority for a 339 grt grab dredger, to be named *Aro*, and it was launched in October 1967.

In 1969 Robbs also purchased equipment from the Burntisland shipyard, which had gone bust; the deal was to take on the men, including one of the directors, along with two busfuls of workers to be transferred back and forth between Leith and Fife each day.

The following are some thoughts and reminiscence from Robert Rowbottom on the merger between Henry Robb and Caledon:

> My memory goes back to late 1968. Mr Robb (the son) had died just as the marriage with Caledon had materialised. Sad in a way, but was this an omen?

For the next 13 years we cooperated with the Caledon yard, just as the Chapman report said we would. This was a government report by Prof. Chapman, which encouraged yards to merge in the interests of efficiency. The senior technical staff moved to Dundee, including Henry Robb Junior, who became joint manager of the merged yard along with someone called Parnell, his Dundee colleague.

And so life went on reasonably pleasantly. There were no redundancies in the design offices. The early estimating and design work was carried out in Dundee, along with the planning for both yards. The commercial headquarters were also at Dundee. Production and development design were carried out independently at both yards. As Assistant Naval

Left: *Eigamoiya* in New Zealand 1989 (G. Ferguson collection).
Right: *Eigamoiya* running trials in the Firth of Forth.

Architect at the time, I had to travel up and down to procure the preliminary estimate information and design particulars, to enable the work to progress in Leith. On the whole the procedure worked quite well until late 1981 when the government decided we would now operate independently as Henry Robb, Leith. But as my memory goes back I think the Dundee design office was kept open to help us until 1984 when … the curtains came down. Many people thought that the merger had contributed to the demise of both yards, but I'm not sure if this was so. I always got on well with, and cooperated with, my colleague Alistair Tosh, the Naval Architect at Dundee. I was travelling up and down to London for meetings with the National Physical Laboratory (test tank), along with the owners and government civil servants.

Shipbuilding continued at the Leith yard with the construction of the fine-looking MV *Eigamoiya*, Ship No 504, the first ship to be launched under the new company name of Robb Caledon Shipbuilders & Engineers Ltd.

This ship had been ordered by the Local Government Council of Nauru. Her principal dimensions were as follows – length overall 367 feet 10 inches with her breadth at 55 feet 2 inches and depth of 30 feet 6 inches. She was powered by twin diesel oil 6-cylinder 4SA engines driving her single shaft, to produce around 5,040 bhp. Her engines were built and supplied by Mirrlees National Ltd, Stockport. Her registered tonnage was given as 4,436 grt when she was launched in December 1968. Her fitting out was completed in April 1969.

She provided good service to the island before going to shipping concerns in Belize in 1993, when she was renamed *Chrysanthi*; and then, flying under the flag of Honduras in 1994, she was renamed once more: *Windsor III*. She was to be renamed yet one more time, to *Asoka II* in 1997. She was deleted from Lloyd's Register in 2011, as her existence was said to be in doubt.

A very welcome order this was, as she was a large order for the yard. She was designed – I have it on good authority – using the previous ships *Hebe* and *Bacchus* as templates for her original lines. But her launching seemed to have caused a bit of argument between some of the old shipwrights.

You see, she was to be launched using a coconut (the second ship to be launched at Leith using a coconut). Not for *Eigamoiya* the traditional bottle of sparkling plonk!

It seems that the bloody coconut didn't break across her bow – indeed, it broke off its line and landed at the bottom of the launching platform. By the time the ship was gliding down the sliding ways, words from the head foreman shipwright were by all accounts heard to the effect of 'get that f**king coconut into the water'.

So it fell to one of the intrepid shipwrights (the closest to the coconut) to pick up the unbroken nut and run down the debris-strewn slipway, dodging all kinds of obstacles, to get close enough to the water to throw the coconut into the sea just after the ship had got there, and so save face with the native chiefs present at the launch. And much to the hilarity of the workforce – it must have been some sight to see this old shipwright, of course not renowned for doing the 100-yard dash, running down the slip shouting 'Get oot ma f**kin way!' But he managed it all the same.

There were a lot of other laughs in a shipyard working environment, some intentional and some not so intentional.

So the good ship *Eigamoiya* was safe into the water, ready to be outfitted and do her trials before being handed over to her owners.

As it turned out, by all accounts she was not a great seakeeping ship in the long rollers of the Pacific, as she had a lot of flare at the bow, and this meant she did a lot of slamming into the seas, which is not very comfortable over any length of time.

Nevertheless, she had many good memories for former crew, as can be seen below from some of the correspondence received about this ship.

Dale Collins:

Good to hear *Eigamoiya* mentioned. Some of the people I sailed with have made the comment that they would do it all over again, even without being paid – that is the sort of free-and-easy life style it was, when working for the Nauruans. The food was very good, and for me as an engineer, it was great to be given the full responsibility of the running and repair of the ship's engine rooms without any bureaucratic interference from head office. Everything was done by word of mouth, which is the islanders' way, and when you joined a ship your reputation was well known. Anyone who had problems while working on the Nauru Pacific Line ships usually incurred those problems by their own actions.

Stryker Solomon:

I sailed on the *Eigamoiya* between 1971 and 1975. Never changed my ship to other Nauruan vessel because my enjoyment of this ship.

Les Costello:

I sailed as fourth engineer on the *Eigamoiya* from 1969 to 1970, joining shortly after it arrived in Melbourne. Coming from British (Conference Line) ships with food

Hedwin (photo from own collection).

GRAB DREDGER "HEDWIN".
146'-6" × 38' × 15'-3"
DISPLT 1600   BHP 1260   V = 10.3
JUNE 1969.

allowance at five shillings per man per day, perhaps it was astonishing to be served steak, scallops etc ... Ports of call were Port Moresby, Lae, Rabaul, Nauru, Melbourne, Geelong and Newcastle – and one run to Japan for the first dry docking. She rolled badly with phosphate load, and the compressed-air remote engine controls were problematic. We were well looked after by the shipping company.

Ship No 505 was an order from the Tyne Ports Authority, Newcastle. She was to be named *Hedwin* (ON 305470), a single-screw grab hopper dredger of 666 grt, another of the complex and special types of ship that the yard had a good name for building.

Her principal dimensions were given as follows – length overall 157 feet 4 inches, with a moulded beam of 39 feet and a moulded depth of 12 feet. She was powered by a diesel oil 6-cylinder 2SA engine, producing around 1,260 bhp to her single shaft. Her engine was built and supplied by British Polar Engines Ltd, Glasgow. She was launched from Robbs in March 1969, and completed in June 1969.

Hedwin was another in the long list of dredgers built by Robbs. These specialities – these one-off complex ships – provided a lot of work for the men in the yard.

The grab hopper dredger *Hedwin* under tow by *Comarco Osprey*, slowly moving down the Tyne on her way to start a new working life in Africa in March 2011.

The *Hedwin* was an order from the Tyne Ports Authority. I remember, as a first-year apprentice, doing a 1/10 scale model of her midships complete with her large hopper tanks; when we had finished, the *Edinburgh Evening News* came down to take a picture and run a story on it.

She was a fair size for a dredger – and, suffice it to say, built and designed for work, not for her looks.

Hedwin was used to keep the River Tyne clear for the many ships using this important waterway, and she was a well-known sight on the river for many years. Indeed, I have found out that it was only at some time in 2010 that she was sold off, after a total of 42 years working the river.

Thanks to Derrick Johnson we know that she was sold off to work in West Africa. With the proper maintenance she could well keep working for many years yet. Derrick has also supplied us with some photographs of her leaving the Tyne – somewhat reluctantly, it would seem, until they got a line on her from the pilot boat.

At the time of writing she is still working away down there in Africa, now under the name of KMC *Pelican,* the name her new owners, Kenya Marine Contractors Ltd, Zanzibar, gave her in 2011.

The build of the *Hedwin* was followed by the tanker MV *Port Tudy*, Ship No 506 (IMO 6922773) in September that year – a somewhat unusual ship order, in that her cargo was not to be oil but French wine, a very important and valuable cargo – some of the men wondered at the time if she might ever be used to bring Beaujolais Nouveau from France into Leith each October/November. She was an order from the French shipping line Soflumar. It is also interesting that her dimensions were given in metric, because the yard, and indeed the whole of the UK, was now moving away from the imperial measurement system to join mainland Europe in using the metric system of measurement.

Her given dimensions when launched from the Robbs yard in September 1969 were as follows – length B.P. 94 metres, with a moulded beam of 15.6 metres and a moulded depth of 8 metres. She was powered by a diesel oil 4SA 2 × 6-cylinder engine driving her single shaft to produce around 3,380 bhp. Her engine was built and supplied by English Electric Diesels Ltd,

Ruston Division, Lincoln. Her registered tonnage when built was given as 3,072 grt. She would be registered in the port of Dunkirk, France.

Sold on by Soflumar in 1994 and renamed *Possidonia*, to be registered in Valletta, Malta, she would be further renamed in 1997 as *Ocean Challenger*, still in Malta, before ending up with

Port Tudy doing her speed trials on the measured mile in the River Forth, February 1970.

Left: MV *Speedway* on sea trials in 1970 (image from own collection).
Right: RRS *Bransfield* carving out a berth for herself in the ice
shelf of Antarctica (photo by Graham Mawdsley).

new owners in Lagos, Nigeria, where at the time of writing she is believed to be still in service, moving oil around.

As the men in the shipyard were now getting their heads around the new metric system the next ship on the stocks was the vehicle transporter *Speedway,* Ship No 507 (IMO 7011462); she was an order from the Elder Dempster Shipping Line.

Her dimensions, when she was launched in February 1970, were given as follows – length B.P. 81 metres with a moulded beam of 16.5 metres and a moulded depth of 4 metres. She was powered by a diesel 4SA 12-cylinder oil engine producing 3,016 bhp to her single shaft. Her engine was built and supplied by W.H. Allen, Son & Co. Ltd, Bedford. Her registered tonnage was given as 1,160 grt, and she was first registered in the port of Liverpool.

MV *Speedway* would go on to have many different owners and name changes, beginning with *Clearway* not long after being taken on by her new owners after successful sea trials in the Forth. She was sold on in 1978 and renamed *O'Shea Express*. In 1984 she would be sold to shipping interests in Beirut, and converted to take livestock – and 'jumboised' in the process to increase her registered tonnage to 4,592 grt. She would carry live cargo for many more years, while her name was changed once more in 2009 to *Ahmed N*. She was last registered in Zanzibar, is and believed to have been broken up at Alang in 2017.

Speedway was followed at the end of the same year by a very special ship, RSS *Bransfield,* Ship No 508.

FOUR
BREAKING THE ICE:
RRS *BRANSFIELD*

Bransfield arrives at Maggie's Ditch in Antarctica (photo by Graeme Hart).

The ice breaker RRS *Bransfield*, 4,816 grt (1,577 tons net), Ship No 508 (IMO 7029079), was designed by consultants Graham & Woolnough of Liverpool (who had designed *Speedway*, Ship No 507), built by Robbs, and launched on 4 September 1970. After fitting out and sea trials in early January 1971 she was ready to be handed over to her proud new owners, the Natural Environment Research Council (NERC). She would be registered in Port Stanley, Falkland Islands.

When I started at Robbs she was in the fitting-out basin, being finished. This basin always held the same depth of water, the dock gates at Leith being in use by this time, and it meant that ships could be launched at Leith without needing to wait on the tide.

RRS *Bransfield* in dry dock at Bethlehem Shipyard, Baltimore, showing the shape of her stem, designed to aid getting through the ice (photo by Clive Sweetingham).

Bransfield was an ice-strengthened cargo ship of Lloyd's 100 A1 Ice Class 1 classification. Her length was 325 feet, her beam 60 feet and her draught 22 feet, with a service speed of 13.5 knots on two engines. She had a cargo capacity of 3,450 cubic metres, with research laboratories, a conference and computer room, and a fully equipped hospital bay on board. Her single screw was powered by a diesel 4SA 2 × 8-cylinder engine, driving electric motors, producing around 6,400 bhp. Her engine had been built and supplied by Mirrlees Blackstone Ltd, Stockport.

Her duties, following the annual discharge of cargo at Halley Station, were to supply and transport cargo and personnel to coastal depots, and to support coastal survey and geological research parties, principally in the region of the Antarctic Peninsula.

During her Atlantic crossing from Southampton to North America in 1974, prior to heading south to Antarctica, hurricane force winds damaged her rudder post. She remained in dry dock for three weeks while repairs were undertaken.

RRS *Bransfield* was British Antarctic Survey's main supply vessel for 29 years, from 1970/71 to 1998/99.

She was the second survey ship to be named after Edward Bransfield RN (1785–1852), who had discovered the north-west coast of the Antarctic Peninsula, and had surveyed the South Shetland Islands, claiming King George Island and Clarence Island for Great Britain. He was the first man to chart part of the Antarctic mainland. (NB The first HMS *Bransfield* was used in Operation Tabarin, a secret British expedition to Antarctica during the Second World War, which established the first permanent British bases on the Antarctic Peninsula. In 1945 they became the Falkland Islands Dependencies, renamed BAS in 1962.)

For much of *Bransfield*'s career her joint masters were John Cole and Stewart Laurence. In 1977 she represented NERC at Spithead in the Review of the Fleet held to celebrate Queen Elizabeth II's jubilee.

The *Bransfield*, or 'Branny' as the men and women who sailed on her used to call her, was a special ship designed and built for special work in some of the toughest weather conditions in the world.

The ravages of the Southern Ocean could batter a less well-equipped ship into an early visit to the breaker's yard – as had, a few years earlier, been found out by two ex-Robbs Loch Class ships working with the New Zealand Navy as weather/lookout ships for aircraft going to Antarctica. After a few years in the conditions down there the ships had suffered so much damage to their hulls that they were removed from service.

The *Bransfield* was strengthened with an ice-breaking bow, which meant that as well as her normal frame spacing she had intermediate framing. This, coupled with the shape of her

Left: *Bransfield* smashes through the pack ice.
Right: *Bransfield* ties up at Maggie's Ditch 1994–95 (photo by Graeme Hart).

FBC on the sea ice in February 1994, with the *Bransfield* in the distance (photo by Graeme Hart).

stem, would allow her to ride up onto pack ice and use her forward movement and weight to break through it.

She was the only ship in the British Isles equipped to go to the frozen regions of the world – and now, with the discovery of oil in the Arctic Ocean, and of course with the possibility of cargo ships using that route, ice breakers will become more important. For years the UK has had to rely on a converted Norwegian ship to represent her interests in the region. But now the interests of the UK will be ongoing, with the 2018 launch of a brand new built-for-purpose vessel from Cammell Laird, named (no, not *Boaty McBoatface!*) the *Sir David Attenborough*.

RRS *Bransfield* had a service life of around 29 years in the most punishing environment imaginable for wear and tear on a ship. The fact that she lasted so long is a testament to her builders and to the crews who maintained her over her working career.

In May 1999 she was sold to Rieber Shipping A/S as part of the contract for the long-term charter of her replacement, RRS *Ernest Shackleton*. She was renamed *Igen Pearl*, and went to the breaker's yard at Mumbai in January 2000.

ANTARCTIC SURVEY STORY

As told by Graeme Hart, British Antarctic Survey Team member.

My uncle was a foreman in a yard in Southampton and as it turned out, he used to refit *Bransfield* years ago. When I told him I was sailing to Antarctica from Grimsby he said 'Not on the *Bransfield* I hope!' He was joking. She was a fine ship, though nearing the end of her service, and I think she needed a bigger and bigger refit each year. I distinctly remember sailing from Grimsby to Tyneside on the Branny for the refi while I was being trained on the meteorological equipment. When we arrived she was put into dry dock, and I was surprised to see that the red paint ended at the waterline.

Months later, when we were sailing through the sea ice in the Weddell Sea, I saw the red paint that they had replaced at Tyneside on all the sea ice in our wake. I guess it was obvious when you think about it – but it looked odd to see the sea ice rubbing the paint off the ship. I had assumed that they had ice-proof paint, bearing in mind that she was an ice-strengthened ship.

Bransfield lowers the cargo tender *Tula* at Maggie's Ditch 1994 (photo by Graeme Hart).

Bransfield at Coronation Island (photo by Graeme Hart).

Left: Driving from Maggie's Ditch with *Bransfield* in the distance, late summer 1995 (photo by Graeme Hart).

Right: *Bransfield* at South Orkney Islands.

Left: *Bransfield* at Husvik, South Georgia Island (photo by Graeme Hart).

Right: *Bransfield* leaves Maggie's Ditch at the end of summer 1994–95

After off-loading cargo at Signy in the South Orkneys the forward cargo hold was quite empty. We put up a table tennis table and used to play ping pong in there; as the ice scraped the hull either side of us it was quite eerie. The ping pong didn't really last long, as every time the ship rammed a sheet of sea ice it all went wrong and we lost the ball under a crate. It was also rather cold in there – the sea was below zero.

We got stuck in the ice in November, and were eventually freed by a Russian ice breaker, which was on hire to tourists. We had helped them out by sending our doctor over to help with a patient, and they returned the favour by clearing a path through the ice for us. This was in the Weddell Sea, which is where Shackleton got trapped with the *Endurance* so many years before. Our ordeal only lasted two days – it is hard to imagine what it was like for them.

One of the saddest things I've ever seen – the *Bransfield* disappearing into the distance in February.

One of the happiest things I've ever seen – the *Bransfield* heaving into view in December.

In between those, two to nine months of isolation at Halley.

The following is an account of life in Antarctica, complete with photographs.

THE *BRANSFIELD* AT HALLEY BAY, ANTARCTICA

The RRS *Bransfield* supplied a number of British Antarctic Survey (BAS) bases, on the Antarctic Peninsula and also on South Georgia, Signy Island (in the South Orkneys) and the furthest-south BAS base at Halley Bay in the Weddell Sea. There were few jetties on which to unload cargo directly from the ship, other than the old whaling station at Grytviken on South Georgia, so in most cases everything from wooden crates and drums of fuel up to bulldozer tractors were ferried ashore using the tender and a scow.

However at Halley Bay, which was located on a floating ice shelf with cliffs extending to around 20 or 25 metres above the sea surface, the *Bransfield* made just one relief call each year, and had to make do with unloading onto whatever sea ice or low ice shelf remained after the main winter sea ice had broken out. Ideal conditions consisted of a small area of sea ice remaining locked in between headlands on either side of a fissure in the ice shelf. These fissures would have filled with drift snow during the winter months and formed a ramp from the sea ice up onto the surface of the ice shelf, up which the tractors could tow the cargo sledges for transfer to the Halley Bay base.

In advance of the ship's arrival, the base personnel would reconnoitre the local coast to identify potential unloading points, but the ship would often have to search further afield (sometimes in excess of 40 kilometres) from the base to find a suitable location. These long journeys meant that the relief could take many days to accomplish, and deteriorating ice conditions might mean that the ship had to be prepared to relocate at short notice in the middle of the exercise. 24-hour daylight assisted the operation, but drifting snow and poor visibility could also prolong the relief operation.

The *Bransfield* would often have to use her ice-strengthened bow to carve out a suitable ice edge, and then the crew would have to haul mooring lines some distance across the ice and attach them to a Deadman anchoring point dug into the ice.

The Halley Bay relief was a rough time for the *Bransfield*, not only carving out her own berth, but also suffering the occasional tonnes of ice falling from the ice cliff onto her deck and rails, resulting in many a 'bit of bent metal'.

My association with the *Bransfield* spanned the period November 1974 to May 1977. As temporary crew on our way to the various bases operated by the BAS we were expected to undertake a number of duties during the voyage. These included not just the normal watch-keeping, weather observations, cleaning etc., but also countless hours on deck chipping rust spots away and, whenever the weather permitted, priming and re-painting. This latter activity was a particular feature of our return trip in early 1977 in preparation for her appearance in the Spithead Review for the Queen's silver jubilee in June of that year.

Graham Mawdsley
BAS Meteorologist,
Halley Bay (Base Z) over-wintering team 1975 and 1976

Unloading from her forward hold (photo by Graham Mawdsley).

Left: *Bransfield*, nosing into the ice to make her berth – interesting to see one of the base crew going up the rope ladder at the bow (photo by Graham Mawdsley).

Middle: Quayside at Halley Bay, showing the small area of habitation in a landscape of ice (photo by Graham Mawdsley).

Lower: RRS *Bransfield* during her sea trials January 1971 (image from own collection).

FIVE
MT *LLOYDSMAN*

The next ship was at the time of her launch one of the most powerful, if not *the* most powerful, tug to be built.

MT *Lloydsman*, Ship No 509 (IMO 7048594) was launched in February 1971. The five-year period starting with that event was a great time for me to be building ships at Leith, not just because I had begun my working life in shipbuilding at that time, but also because some very interesting ships were being built.

Lloydsman was very active during her working life, and she even took part in protecting British fishing vessels during what became known as the Cod Wars, a series of disputes over fishing rights between Iceland and the UK. Her specifications and dimensions were impressive – length B.P. 67.21 metres, with a moulded beam of 14.172 metres, and moulded depth at 8.5 metres. She was powered by a diesel oil 4SA 2 × 10-cylinder Pielstick, producing a massive 10,000 bhp to her single shaft. Her engine was built and supplied by Crossley Engineering Co. Ltd, Manchester. Her registered tonnage was given at 2,041 grt when launched by Robbs, and she would be registered at Hull. She was managed by Humber Tugs Ltd of Hull, which was to be her home base.

She had been ordered by the famous towing company Union Towing Co Ltd, a company with a long and proud tradition of ship towage and doing the jobs that few others would attempt. When the company needed the best it was the Leith yard that they turned to, as the yard had built many, many fine tugs since its inception in 1918. The *Lloydsman* was a special ship with a special power system installed, namely her Towmaster propulsion and steering system.

The following is condensed from a promo written by David Rowlands just after *Lloydsman* had been handed over to the Union Towing Company in 1971:

United Towing have introduced a mighty contender in the ocean towing stakes, the *Lloydsman*. Bristling with salvage gear, radio antennae and navigation aids, United Towing's new 16,000-horsepower tug is capable of handling the largest ships and oil rigs. *Lloydsman*, designed by Burness Corlett Partners, patrols the world's shipping lanes listening out around the clock for distress signals or the news of a hard-won towing contract. *Lloydsman* challenges,

Above: The ocean-going salvage tug
MT *Lloydsman*, seen here at Gibraltar.

Right: The supertug *Lloydsman* in Leith dry
dock after her first six months. Note the
complex Towmaster propulsion and steering
system; a 17-foot Kamewa controllable-
pitch propeller and five steering vanes, two
for'ard and three aft of the prop tube (photo
by Pete Bass, shown here by permission).

in power and range of operation, three mighty tugs owned by the West German operator
Bugsier.

'The dominance of West German and Dutch operators in the field of ocean salvage is a
very successful myth put about by their publicity agents and the British press,' says the man
at the helm of Hull-based United Towing, Britain's only contenders in the offshore towing
business. Playing it cool is managing director Tony Wilbraham's ploy, because that's the way
the customers like it – he could back his claim with impressive lists of tonnages and valuable
cargoes rescued but prefers not to. You understand why when you realise that some of his
most contented clients are oil companies whose ships have the habit of creating international
panics at the first whiff of helplessness on the seas.

Admittedly Bugsier, the largest West German ocean salvage company, has three giant tugs
– *Oceanic*, *Arctic* and *Pacific* – each of 17,500 hp, and all capable of handling the largest
super-tankers with ease. Since last October they have been challenged by United Towing's
Lloydsman – not on the face of it, at 16,000 hp quite in the same league, but, owing to a
unique propulsion and steering system, able to undertake equally exacting jobs. *Lloydsman*
was designed by Burness, Corlett & Partners, and built at Leith by Robb Caledon Shipbuilders
Ltd.

The Towmaster principle is to enclose the ship's propeller in a fixed nozzle, and replace
the normal rudder by aerofoil section vanes fore and aft of the nozzle tube. The system
is completely variable, to suit anything from the smallest in-harbour vessel right up to
Lloydsman. The designers have evolved a computer program incorporating all the relevant
parameters of Towmaster – feed in the design parameters such as bollard pull, free running
speed and manoeuvrability required, plus the amount of engine power you want to install,

and the computer chews out the various optional Towmaster arrangements. Tug design is inevitably a compromise between free running speed, forward and stern steerability, displacement, bollard pull and economy of operation.

'United Towing's specification for *Lloydsman* stretched our program to the fullest,' admits partner J.L. Smettem: 'When you go to the extreme limits of a design like this you have to verify the results by tank testing.' They did this at British Hovercraft's laboratories. A model of *Lloydsman* was subjected to every possible condition she was likely to meet at sea. Wind tunnel tests enabled the architects to fair her massive 17-foot diameter nozzle into the steel hull and modify the design of the Kamewa controlled-pitch propeller rotating inside with only one inch clearance all round. Her bulbous bow, designed to modify the wave pattern of water entering the nozzle, was proved satisfactory, as were the architects' attempts to keep the vessel's stern down at all times. *Lloydsman* has five shutter rudders, two forward and three aft, giving a turning circle of only two and a half ship's-length diameter. She is 262 feet long and has a breadth of 46 feet 6 inches.

Lloydsman is driven by two Crossley Pielstick V10 diesels of 5,000 bhp, each coupled through a Richardson Westgarth gearbox. On just one engine *Lloydsman* has the capability of most ocean-going tugs now in service, with a bollard pull, measured during trials by an independent laboratory at Europoort, Rotterdam, of 80 tons. On both engines the inspectors measured a pull of 135 tons steady, rising to 150 tons maximum. These figures are the indisputable record of Burness, Corlett's achievement, because they are as high as the claimed figures for *Lloydsman*'s German rivals, which don't have the backing of independent trials. In addition, *Oceanic* et al are twin-screw tugs, so single-engined operation is inefficient, while United Towing reckon that most of their work can be done economically on one engine. At full stretch *Lloydsman* can pull a 350,000-ton tanker at 7 knots and can make 18.6 knots running free. Tugmen place a high value on their ships' displacement, reckoning that in certain situations the more like a sea anchor the tug becomes the easier it is to perform its task. Fully loaded, *Lloydsman* has a world-beating displacement of 3,100 tons including 1,500 tons of fuel, enough for 45–50 days' towing at maximum power.

Lloydsman is unique among the world's ocean-going tugs, dominating not by power and speed alone but in overall design and economy of operation – a formidable fighting vessel, capable of dealing with tankers over 500,000 tons and the largest oil-drilling platforms. Tony Wilbraham provides an amusing example of what tugs like *Lloydsman* mean to the world's shipowners: he claims that rather than lay up a damaged tanker for six months' repairs in a dockyard with consequent loss of revenue, it is cheaper for the owner to hire *Lloydsman* as a permanent tow to pull the oil-filled hulk between the Persian Gulf and Europe.

The secret of *Lloydsman*'s performance is the Towmaster propulsion and steering system … developed by the designers for adaption by computer techniques to the needs of various sizes of tug. *Lloydsman*'s Towmaster unit has a 17-foot Kanewa controlled-pitch propeller and five steering vanes, two fore and three aft of the propeller tube, to give adequate manoeuvrability forward and astern.

All in all, quite a vessel, and she was to ply the world's oceans for the Union Towing Company for almost ten years. During that time she was also put to good use to protect Britain's fishing interests when the so-called Icelandic Cod Wars broke out; she was on hand to protect the fishing vessels in the area, who were under considerable pressure from Icelandic gunboats to get the hell out of it.

This deep-sea salvage tug, a principal player in the Cod Wars, was involved in some really nasty moments recorded on film and shown on TV.

ICELANDIC COD WARS

Some background

The so-called Cod Wars were more of a political fight than any actual war – Britain claiming fishing rights near Iceland while Iceland was trying to protect her own – although it was taken very seriously by the two protagonists. They had been arguing about this from the late 1940s until things began to get more serious. The third of these skirmishes between Icelandic gunboats and the Royal Navy happened around the end of 1976; this was when *Lloydsman* became one of the vessels sent to Icelandic waters to help protect the British fishing vessels there.

A lot of livelihoods were at stake, the eventual outcome being catastrophic for the deep-sea fishermen of the UK. Since 1982 a 200-nautical-mile (370-kilometre) exclusive economic zone has been the United Nations standard. So Iceland won the argument, and as a result British fishing communities lost access to the rich fishing areas, a result that devastated the traditional fishing ports such as Hull, Grimsby and Fleetwood with thousands of skilled fishermen and people in related trades being put out of work.

In 2012 the British government offered a multimillion-pound compensation deal and an apology to the fishermen who had lost their livelihoods in the 1970s. More than 35 years after the workers had lost their jobs, the £1,000 compensation offered to 2,500 fishermen was somewhat derisory from a government that just wanted to forget about its past mistakes.

Ægir, one of the Icelandic gunboats, whose captain showed great seamanship and no lack of confidence in taking on the larger tugs and frigates of the Royal Navy.

Left: *Lloydsman* docking at Hull.

Right: The Icelandic gunboat *Thor*. She and *Lloydsman* were always having a go at each other, and although *Lloydsman* was much bigger, this did not deter *Thor* from ramming her once or twice.

Left: An Icelandic gunboat turning to try and intimidate *Lloydsman*'s skipper, Norman Storey.

Right: *Thor* preparing to ram *Lloydsman* (which she then did, resulting in *Lloydsman* having to retire to the Faroes for repairs).

My thanks go to David Lewis for the photographs above.

It was into this melée that a young David Lewis entered, working on the tug *Lloydsman*. He managed to get some photographs while involved in the Cod Wars. He told me, 'When it got close to us I would throw industrial-size bottles of ketchup at it. Being a 17-year-old I didn't worry about it.'

As a tug built at by Robbs, *Lloydsman* had a relatively short working career; perhaps she was just worked into the ground (although this would be an odd description for a ship) – or perhaps, more likely, she just became too costly to keep on standby, with fewer and fewer cargoes to chase for salvage once the Suez Canal was back in business. And with the advent of more and more heavy lift capable ships around the world to carry huge loads over oceans, she was just not needed so much.

She was sold to Selco Salvage Limited of Singapore during 1979, and renamed *Salviscount*. They proceeded to give her an all-white paint job. She was to work out of Singapore as her home base for another eight years or so before being sold for scrapping in Pakistan, in March 1988.

Dated 3rd February 78.

Giant task for the Lloydsman

THE 16,000 horsepower Hull tug Lloydsman has been chartered to tow the collision-damaged giant tanker, Venpet, from Cape Town to Nagasaki in Japan.

The voyage, expected to start tomorrow, will take about 55 days and is a valuable contract for Lloydsman's owners.

Late last year the 152,372 tons Venpet and her sister tanker, Venoil, were in collision off the South African coast and, over Christmas, the Lloydsman helped to tow the Venpet (above) into Cape town for temporary repairs.

The 2,040 tons Lloydsman is the flagship of Ocean Tugs, part of the United Towing Group, and for the tow to Japan where the Venpet will undergo permanent repairs, will be commanded by Capt. Charles Noble, of Hull.

SIX
THE 1970s

The *Lloydsman* was followed by two different orders for ro-ro container ships, the first of them ordered for Common Bros. She was the 3,822 grt MV *Caribbean Progress*, Ship No 510, launched in October 1971.

This was at a time when there was huge interest in cross-North Sea trade, and the ro-ro container ship was the next new concept of this form of transport. And of course this concept was good for trade on any of the world's trade routes.

This in effect meant that a truck and trailer with its container still in place would go as cargo on the ship, or the truck cab would be unhitched and just the trailer would go, to be met at the other side by another cab, to continue on its way.

The following information on the *Caribbean Progress* is provided by Tim Hudson, who was chief engineer on her:

The MV *Caribbean Progress* was intended to trade for a Common Brothers subsidiary in New York, Caribbean Trailer Express. However, this company was already in difficulties by

Caribbean Progress during her sea trials in the Forth (image from own collection).

time of delivery, so the vessel was time-chartered to Co-ordinated Caribbean Transport of Miami.

She traded regularly from that port to Guatemala and Honduras until August 1974 when, after the guarantee docking in Savannah, Georgia, she took up a charter running cars from New Brunswick to Newfoundland. At this time she suffered major main engine mechanical problems following a crankcase explosion.

In 1979 she was chartered by Karageorgis, and she traded across the Adriatic, between Patras and Ancona with ferry traffic, before being sold to a charterer.

I was chief engineer on those three trades, and present at the handing-over ceremony to the Greek owner around 1st April 1979.

Capt John Gyte, c/o John Greenwood, 2nd Eng Neil Anderson.

The ro-ro concept was nothing new to Henry Robb, as the yard had in fact built a couple of ro-ro barges for use in Singapore before the Second World War. (Both barges were scuttled ahead of the advancing Japanese army.)

The *Caribbean Progress* was sold in 1975 to Iranian shipping interests, and she was to be sold on a few more times and converted in 1986 to take more passengers as well as containers. Her gross tonnage went from 3,822 up to 4,469, and she was renamed *Valentino* the same year.

She was eventually sold for her scrap value, and broken up in 2002.

Then it was a long build on the slip for the next ship, to be called MV *Hero*, Ship No 511 (IMO 7217951). She was launched the following year, in December 1972, but she was to meet

Above: *Caribbean Progress* flying the Iranian flag, with a cargo of trucks (image from Wikipedia).

Right: Launch of Ship No 511, MV *Hero* (image from own collection).

with her unfortunate demise in the teeth of a North Sea storm in 1977 while managed by the Wilson Line. She was a ship that had been altered considerably since her launch at Robbs.

The twin screw ro-ro transport ship *Hero* had been an order from a company formed from two very famous ship-owning lines: EWL and DFDS (UK) Ltd.

Domino Container Ships Ltd and the Danish ferry company had decided to collaborate as joint venture partners on some of the routes over the North Sea, hence the new company set up to run the ships, to be managed by the Wilson Line, who ran all their ships out of the home port of Hull. But to all intents and purposes she was an Ellerman Wilson ship.

With the increase in traffic required over the short sea route from the east coast of the British Isles to Scandinavia there was at the time an opening in the market for ship owners to make some real profit out of these routes. The MV *Hero* had room for 12 passengers as well as her crew.

This was the second similar ship to be built at Robbs.

Launched from the yard in 1972, she was another fair-size ship to be built at the yard with, as I remember, a big slab side. It seemed to rise very high from her keel, which rested on the keel blocks; to her main deck was a height of around 40 feet plus 4 feet of keel block clearance, so it was a long way up to get to her superstructure.

Her dimensions when launched were given as follows – length B.P. 105 metres with a moulded breadth of 19 metres and a moulded depth of 12 metres. She was powered by twin Pielstick-Crossley 10PC2V diesels, producing 10,000 hp to her two shafts. Her registered tonnage at launch was given as 3,468 grt. The vessel was to be registered at the port of Hull.

She was to undergo a ship lengthening during 1976 at a Dutch shipyard, so that she could carry more cargo, and the height of her sides was also increased by a further 2 metres or so.

Her length was increased by 18.3 metres, and her gross tonnage went up from 3,468 tonnes to 4,493.

The newly lengthened ship was to ply her trade over the North Sea for a further year or so before she set out on a voyage from Esbjerg in Denmark, heading for Grimsby, on the east coast of England. But after two days of very heavy weather the ship was found to be taking on a lot of water, and her captain decided to abandon ship. The rescue services, including a helicopter from a nearby Canadian Navy ship, HMCS *Huron*, were alerted and at the scene pretty quickly. The helicopter managed to lift seven of the crew of the stricken vessel, but unfortunately one of the crewmen died from the injuries he had received, just as the rescue helicopter landed on the deck of HMCS *Huron* in horrendous weather. The crew of the helicopter are to be commended for taking off in such bad weather, but that is what people at sea do when another vessel is in danger.

Hero sank on the following day, 13 November 1977.

The official inquiry into the foundering of the MV *Hero* found the ship owners at fault for the unseaworthiness of the ship. Here is an extract:

The full minutes and official report of the formal investigation held in Hull over a period of ten days in June/July 1979, into the disaster that befell the M/V HERO in the North Sea with the loss of one seaman, on the 13th of November 1977. Messrs Gurney & Sons provide a word

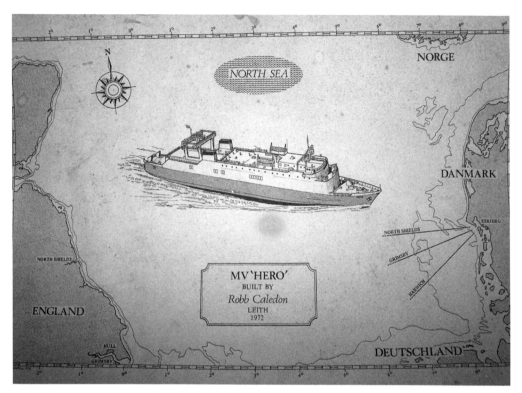

This print was sent to me by Alex Grosset, who as a young lad
sailed on *Hero* many times from Grimsby to Esbjerg.

by word account of the proceedings of the court so a full and complete record is presented. The Court concluded that the loss of the ship was due in part by the continuing ingress of water through the vessel's stern doors due to the un-seaworthy condition, and in part by the further ingress of water probably through heavy weather damage in way of the forecastle deck. The un-seaworthiness was caused by the wrongful act or default of the owners. The HERO was a Ro-Ro vessel registered in Hull and owned jointly by the Domino Container Ships Limited and DFDS (UK) Ltd, both of London. She was originally built in 1972 by Robb Caledon at Leith, and structurally altered in Holland in 1976 when she was lengthened. The HERO sailed on her final voyage from Esbjerg for Grimsby on the 11th of November 1977, laden with about 3,654 tonnes of cargo. Officers and crew totalled 27 and in addition there were 3 passengers on board. Two days out in open sea the ship ran into heavy weather and began to list as she took on water in her engine room and trailer deck. "Immediate assistance" was requested, and the ship was abandoned and later sank.

I sailed with *Hero* many times, with my dad, who worked for DFDS.

When onboard at a young age I was introduced to the Snoopy club, which was a bar onboard and given a print on A3 card of the *Hero* on a map in the North Sea showing her runs with the inscription 'MV *Hero*, built by Robb Caledon Leith 1972'.

MV *Hero* at the Dutch shipyard of ADM, as built by Robb Caledon Shipbuilders, Leith.

Left: MV *Hero* in the floating dock being lengthened (jumboised) at the Dutch shipyard of ADM.
Right: This photo, from the Dutch Ship Museum, shows the MV *Hero* being
converted at the Dutch shipyard of ADM (shown here by kind permission).

The end of 1973 was to see three ships launched into the cold water of the Leith Basin, as ordered by the Ministry of Defence.

RMAS *Goosander*, Ship No 513, was the first into the water, from the front of Berth 3. Her sister ship, built forward of her on the same slipway, was RMAS *Pochard*, Ship No 514; she would be launched in December of the same year, and would create quite a splash, as she was so far from the water and had some way to slide down the slipway before flotation would occur.

Left: *Goosander* at anchor (image credit unknown at present).

Right: RMAS *Goosander* was laid up for some time after this at Brooke Marine in Lowestoft, England, before being sold to commercial interests in the 1990s. She was to ply her trade doing survey and salvage work in the waters off the West African coast.

RMAS *Goosander* (A164) was part of the order from the Admiralty which had seen HMS *Herald* built at Robbs.

Goosander's principal dimensions were given as follows – length overall 58 metres with a beam of 12 metres and a depth of 4 metres. She was powered by a diesel engine producing around 750 bhp to her single shaft. Her engine was built and supplied by Ruston Paxman Diesels Ltd, Colchester. Her registered tonnage was given as 923 grt.

She was launched in April 1973 and completed in September 1973.

She was a mooring and salvage/boom defence vessel of the Wild Duck class. As she was an order for the MoD (Navy) her build was carried out in the imperial measurement system; the Navy had not at that point changed to the metric system which had come into effect in the UK in 1970.

As part of the Royal Maritime Auxiliary Service, she was to be based in her home port of Portsmouth. This capable little ship was designed and built to fulfil many different roles in both peacetime and war – a real working ship.

With her two bow horns she was capable of raising 200 tons from the seabed over her bows.

With a crew of 58 she was also to play a part in the Falklands War; along with a few other Leith-built ships she was part of the task force that retook the islands from the invading Argentine forces in 1982.

She was part of an attempt to save a badly damaged Argentine submarine, the *Santa Fe*, in South Georgia, but due to very heavy weather the attempt was abandoned.

The RMAS *Goosander* was the subject of a TV film crew report for the Scottish News on her return from the Falklands.

In 2006 she was renamed *UTEC Surveyor* (IMO 4500084).

At the time of writing she is still listed as in service, although it is not known which country's flag she flies.

The RMAS

The Royal Maritime Auxiliary Service used to form a major part of the Marine Services organisation which existed to support the Royal Navy. It was a branch of the Ministry of Defence (Naval).

It provided a versatile, flexible and cost-effective service which included harbour tugs and pilots to assist ships of the Fleet when berthing and un-berthing; delivering fuel, water and victualling stores with purpose-built vessels and craft to ships in harbour; transporting ammunition; ferrying personnel to and from ships at anchor or secured to buoys, and providing specially designed vessels for other tasks such as moorings and salvage, torpedo recovery, underwater research and development and degaussing.

All RMAS vessels had a buff-coloured superstructure and black hulls with an all-round white riband at deck level.

Reproduced from the excellent RMAS website, with the kind permission of Brian Westmore.

For more on the RMAS visit http://www.rmasassociation.co.uk/index.html

Quote from an ex-skipper of RMAS *Goosander*

I know Alistair MacGregor, the long-time Master of *Goosander*, was really hacked-off that the SAL class went to Hall Russell in Aberdeen and not to Robbs at Leith in the mid-1980s. He lobbied long and hard, saying that Robbs built a much better ship, but the Admiralty wanted cheap, and in his view that's what they got! When he retired from Salmaster I took over as master for a while, having been mate for two years before that.

As a point of interest, I was skipper on *Goosander* when she transferred to Greenock to replace *Pochard*, and I then took *Pochard* down to Portsmouth for disposal at a later date. Sad to see the old ones going, but *Goosander* is still active as UTEC *Goosander*, I think. They fitted her with a bow thruster and changed her derricks for a hydraulic crane.

Best Regards, Mike

Launch of the RMAS *Goosander*, Ship No 513 (image from own collection).

Such a tough little vessel had a tight-knit crew, and some of their stories are shown below.

Bob Holbrook:

I worked on *Goosander* as cook for two weeks' cover. A great little ship with a good crowd and an enjoyable nice trip. I remember the fridges were down a vertical ladder. I joined her in Newhaven 10/07/01 and left her at Greenwich Lt Buoy 24/07/01. Still at sea after 37 years, but always have fond memories of this one.

Alan Durham:

I was on RMAS *Goosander* as part of Task Force in the Falklands, and am applying for an Atlantic Medal without success, as the crew list and documentation cannot be found. Are you able to advise where this can be obtained, as we have hit a brick wall? I appreciate this may not be your area of expertise, but thought it was worth a try. Many thanks.

Richard Gabriele:

Goosander was until recently called *UTEC Surveyor*, and was doing survey work for the oil industry. Her bow apron was altered to cope with small seismic wires, and she had more deck equipment fitted. She was registered in Kingston (St Vincent & Grenadines).

She is still named *UTEC Surveyor*, and is presently operated by Maltese interests. She is on a wreck removal operation of a 40-metre fishing vessel which sank at her berth after being rammed by a cargo ship last week in Valletta.

Mike Farmer:

I was lucky to have served as an engineer on *Goosander* from 1984 to 1987, which included the successful salvage of the *Santa Fe* from Grytviken Bay, South Georgia (1984/85). It was certainly a challenge for all on board, especially during the voyage to and from South Georgia. We were exposed to horrendous sea conditions at times (severe gales, fog, icebergs), but I can recall we had a few laughs on the way, too. The *Goosander* was never really intended for such epic travel, but thanks to a brilliant crew we all came back in one piece, having achieved a successful mission.

Tam Scott:

I was part of the crew who carried out the salvage of the Argentine submarine *Santa Fe*. As one of the younger members of the crew I was looked after by the older members, and always look back with fondness and will never forget the camaraderie we shared.

SEVEN
HMS *HERALD*

HMS *Herald*, Ship No 512, was the second down the slipway from Berth 2. She was launched in October 1973 after some two years on the berth due to many problems, by way of both unrest in the yard and the MoD's constant requirement for changes to the ship.

HMS *Herald* was an order from the MoD Navy for a hydrographic survey ship to be built at Robbs.

Her principal dimensions were given as follows – length B.P. 235 feet with a moulded beam of 49 feet and a moulded depth of 25 feet 9 inches. Her registered tonnage was given as 2,533 grt. She was powered by three 12-cylinder Paxman Ventura engines for the diesel-electric main propulsion, and two 6-cylinder Venturas driving auxiliary gensets. She had a service speed of 14 knots.

She seemed to take forever to build, and she was on the stocks for those two years mainly due to changes that were forced on the yard by the Navy team in attendance there – no sooner would a deck level be complete than along they would come and insist that, due to all the constantly changing gear that she was being fitted with, this deck or that bulkhead would have to come out or be moved.

In addition, Yarrows, a rival yard on the Clyde, had built the previous four in the class, and had many of the drawings that were required for *Herald*'s build. But Yarrows were somewhat miffed at the MoD, as they thought they alone were entitled to be awarded the contract for what would be the fifth ship ordered for the hydrographic survey fleet. Even though this annoyance was only to be expected from another yard in what was a very competitive business with fewer and fewer orders to be won, getting the drawings and any other information from them took many weeks at a time. All this did not help with the build schedule.

Herald was fitted with a bow thrust door – a sliding door, port and starboard, which could be raised and lowered when required. Bow thrust doors would give a streamlined shell when lowered and sealed in position.

Herald was a ship that I remember very well, as this was one of the first jobs I worked on in the loft. When told to report to one of the journeymen, Peter Rennie, who was laying out the doors full size on the loft floor, I remember going out to look at this mass of lines going

Above: HMS *Herald* safely taken in tow after her launch, sitting very true on the water.

Left: HMS *Herald* launched into the Western Harbour at Leith, shipwrights looking on now they have done their part.

Below: HMS *Herald* served with distinction all over the world and she was used as a hospital evacuation ship during the Falklands War, then with leading minesweeping squadrons in the Iraq War.

everywhere, and Peter asking me if I knew what I was looking at. My reply was no – and he replied to me that neither did he! Now, to get more than two sentences out of Peter was an accomplishment, but what this man did not know about lofting just wasn't worth knowing. And so the work started. In further talks about the bow thruster doors much later, while in correspondence with one of *Herald*'s captains, he informed me that the Navy had got so fed up with the problems caused by the doors that they eventually just got them removed, and the bow thruster tunnel was then faired into the shell.

Don't get me wrong – they were some bit of design work, and also a tremendous job to loft and fabricate. I am not 100 per cent certain, as it was some time ago, but I seem to recollect that the doors were prefabricated by Brown Brothers Ltd of Edinburgh, a company well known for the supply of items for ships such as stabilisers. The doors would have been supplied with the developed shell plates, and Browns would have fabricated the stiffening of the doors along with all the hydraulics and seals etc. The finished doors would then be returned to the shipyard for fitting into the bow.

But to expect these heavy fabricated doors, working on hydraulics, to be able to seal after use in some of the worst sea conditions to be found in the world was perhaps expecting just a bit too much.

I never did fully understand the design of the doors, and even back then they did seem a bit over the top for what they were intended to do.

I also made a one-tenth-scale model of her stern, and had to develop out her cant frames as she had a nice rounded stern – the kind that you don't see any more today, as it is much too complicated and expensive to construct. Now they go for flat slab transom sterns, nice and easy to fabricate.

She had other different build methods used on her, as she also had an all-aluminium superstructure. It gave some good shapes at the time, but it was filthy stuff for the men to work with. And the aluminium was to prove very vulnerable on other Royal Navy ships when hit during the Falklands conflict. She also had a helicopter hangar at the after end of the main deck.

HMS *Herald* also had fitted a very fine teak deck. This took the shipwrights ages, as there was so much of it – but what a cracking job they made of it, and when they had finished it just looked like a deck on a fancy liner. It almost felt criminal to be lining off and fitting the ship's datum plates on this deck.

She was the first ship that I worked on that had a jail built into the foc'sle. It was just aft of the huge chain locker, so anyone in there, with a few hundred yards of anchor chain rattling past their head, would know exactly when the ship had arrived and dropped anchor.

I always thought that she was a fine-looking ship, and she was duly launched from the Berth 1 (East). By this time the yard had only three berths to build and launch ships from, down from the nine that they had at the end of the Second World War.

HMS *Herald* slid into the sea down the sliding ways on 4 October 1973, and was tied up at the fitting-out basin to be completed.

HMS *Herald*, seen under way in this photograph sent to me by her commanding officer, I.M. Bartholomew.

Sea trials commenced in the Firth of Forth on 28 Aug 1974, and she was formally accepted by the MoD Navy on 31 October. After commissioning in Portsmouth on 22 November, she undertook a shakedown cruise in the Bay of Biscay, followed by a work-up prior to Christmas.

The following is a condensed version of a booklet sent to me some time ago by I.M. Bartholomew, Commander Royal Navy, the then commanding officer of HMS *Herald*, on the occasion of her celebrating 21 years of service in the Royal Navy in 1995.

HMS *Herald* had a distinguished service life, starting with her survey work in and around the British Isles. In particular with regard to supporting the offshore oil industry, she worked in the Mediterranean, West Africa and the Persian Gulf, where in 1979 she evacuated British and foreign nationals from Iran.

After serving as a hospital ship during the Falklands campaign, HMS *Herald* was converted to the ice patrol ship role, and worked in the South Atlantic between 1983 and 1987.

Halfway through her 1988 refit, it was decided that the ship should be converted to undertake the MCM (mine countermeasure) command and support role, and she deployed to the Gulf in that role for 15 consecutive months in 1989–90.

In late February 1991, at the climax of the Gulf War, she was in the van of the naval forces assembled off Kuwait.

She then reverted to her survey role in the Atlantic Ocean, conducting oceanographic and geophysical surveys.

HMS *Herald* made a significant contribution to national and coalition naval operations in peace and war, and proved to be a very adaptable ship.

Above: The Paxman Ventura engine similar to the one fitted into HMS *Herald*. She had three of them (photo from the Paxman History website).

Upper left: HMS *Herald* seen from above (photo credit unknown).

Left: *Herald* under way

Four ships: HMS *Hecla* (A133), HMS *Hecate* (A137), and HMS *Hydra* (A144) were built by Yarrow & Co of Glasgow in 1965–66. HMS *Herald* (H138) was built by Robb Caledon and completed in 1974.

LOA 79 metres, beam 15.4 metres; speed 14 knots.

Engines: three 12YCZ (Ventura) main engines, each rated 1,165 bhp at 1,250 rpm, and two 6YJXZ auxiliaries, per ship.

The British Royal Navy was an important customer for the Ventura. Four hydrographic survey vessels, HMS *Herald*, HMS *Hecate*, HMS *Hydra* and HMS *Hecla*, were each equipped with three 12-cylinder Venturas for their diesel-electric main propulsion, and two 6-cylinder Venturas driving auxiliary gensets. Early Type 22 Frigates each had four 16-cylinder Venturas for electrical power generation (12-cylinder Valentas were used for the Batch 3 Type 22s).

The first surveying task in *Herald*'s life was in the Mediterranean, for which she sailed from Portsmouth in January 1975. The passage out was in the teeth of a south-westerly gale, which not only delayed her arrival at Gibraltar but also proved to be a forerunner of the weather for the rest of the year.

Three months were spent in the Med, Malta being the ship's base before she returned to home waters, to carry out surveys around the north of Scotland.

In 1976, after a refit at HM Naval Base, Portsmouth, HMS *Herald* sailed for the north of Scotland again, to continue her work on the survey grounds north-east of the Shetland Isles.

The surveys were carried out by boat and the ship's Wasp helicopter, and while the main problem was generally the violent weather conditions, the ship's seakeeping qualities and extensive storage facilities proved invaluable.

Above: *Herald*'s flight deck; en route to Ghana in 1978.

Left: Lieutenant A.l. Cole and Leading Aircrewman Wellman-Matthews at Achowa Hi-fix site.

During February 1977 the ship was involved in the salvage of MV *El Tambo* after that vessel had been abandoned by her crew with almost 1,000 head of cattle on board; a major fire had broken out in the engine room and had spread through the after part of the ship.

Two members of *Herald*'s company were decorated for gallantry during the rescue.

HMS *Herald* also took part in the silver jubilee review of the fleet that year.

The following year, 1978, was to see the ship in West African waters, and on her return to Portsmouth she went into dry dock for work on the leaking seals of her bow thrust unit.

The following photographs, sent to me by Lt Cmdr A. Cole, show the *Herald*'s Wasp helicopter in use during visits to Ghana.

Towards the end of the year *Herald* was to go into dry dock again, this time for conversion to an ice patrol ship, and she was fitted with guns for the first time, with 2 × 20 mm Oerlikons on her bridge wings. She was also converted to permit night flying operations.

The next year was to see HMS *Herald* in the waters around the Persian Gulf, where she undertook many surveys, interrupted for a time by the need to evacuate British nationals and others from Iran and take them to Dubai after the uprising against the Shah.

The next two years were to entail survey work back in the north of Scotland, then back to the Persian Gulf, and also a trip down to Mombasa before the call was received that she was required for duty in the Falklands War.

This was in April 1982, and she was quickly converted to an ambulance ship. Red crosses were painted on all her visible surfaces, and the removal of some of her gear was undertaken, along with the fitting of a stump mast to enable her to refuel at sea.

Herald arrived off the Falklands on 26 May, joining the SS *Uganda*, HMS *Hecla* and HMS *Hydra* in the Red Cross Box, north of Falklands Sound.

On 8 June, 60 casualties were embarked on *Herald* from *Uganda*, and transported to Montevideo.

Herald then returned to the Falklands to take on a further 100 casualties from *Uganda*, some of them stretcher cases, and transport them to Montevideo. She then embarked on her return trip to the UK.

She returned to Portsmouth on 21 July, to a moving and unforgettable welcome.

She was destined for six months of patrol in the South Atlantic, working turnabout with HMS *Endurance*.

Her small ship's boats were sheathed in wood, to enable them to operate in the ice.

And so her survey and patrol work continued on into 1984, when in March she was to carry HRH Prince Andrew on an official visit to St Helena, to celebrate the island having been a crown colony for 150 years.

Then it was back to the stormy waters of the South Atlantic, to carry on with her survey work, and so it was for a further two years, only one of the trips to the Falklands being carried out in the summer months. Then in August 1984 it was time for her to make a westward passage round Cape Horn, then north to the Panama Canal, with a few stops on the way.

Then with an overnight transit through the Panama Canal and a quick jaunt around the Caribbean, across the Atlantic to Devonport, arriving on 5 October.

There was a further visit to the South Atlantic to carry out survey work again, carried out in the southern hemisphere's winter season, then *Herald* returned to the UK on 1 December 1985 for a well-earned break.

Then it was back to surveying Scottish waters for the first half of 1986, before being called to go back down to the Falklands as HMS *Endurance* was due for a major refit in Portsmouth.

So it was to the stormy waters of the South Atlantic she was destined, but on this voyage to the South Atlantic, her work would for the one and only time be carried out in the summer season.

Then, as she arrived back in her now home port of Devonport she was to be repainted back to her all-white surveying livery.

So in for another refit. It was around this time that it was decided that this versatile ship would be converted to replace HMS *Abdiel* as the MCM (mine counter-measure) command and support vessel in the Gulf.

Her flight deck was strengthened and lengthened to support Lynx helicopter operations, even though that aircraft would never fit inside the hangar.

The temptation to paint the ship grey again was, however, resisted.

Herald was deployed in the Gulf region for the next 15 months, and did not arrive back at Devonport until April 1989.

Then the first eight months of 1990 were spent in and around the Norwegian Sea until on 2 August 1990 Iraq invaded Kuwait, and it was decided that a UK MCM force, with *Herald* as the MCM command and support ship, should be dispatched to the Gulf region.

In Jan 1991, when hostilities against Iraq commenced, the ship was engaged in MCM support operations, including paving and confirming the way for the US Navy battleships, which were to provide naval gunfire support for the land battle in Kuwait.

Whilst conducting MCM support operations the ships came under Silkworm missile attack from Kuwait, but the missile was shot down by HMS *Gloucester* without causing any damage.

On 1 March *Herald* handed over her role to HMS *Hecla* and headed back home. She then commenced her refit programme, which was extended due to more problems with the bow thrust.

Left: HMS *Herald* in her grey Navy livery as the command and support ship for mine countermeasures.
Right: HMS *Herald* at anchor

Herald returning home.

1992 started with the ship back on her surveying duties, although she was now having some problems with her main engines. However, she headed for the central Atlantic, and traversed it from Dakar to Brazil. Then back to the UK to have her centre and starboard engines replaced before heading off on a flag visit to St Petersburg, Russia.

She was to continue crossing the Atlantic for the next couple of years, taking all that the violent seas and sometimes hurricane force winds could throw at her.

She was to have further problems with her bow thruster doors, but throughout 1995 continued to carry out her survey work in the Atlantic, with some NATO exercises in between.

She was to take centre stage during the celebrations in London's West India Dock to mark the 200th anniversary of the founding of the Hydrographic Office. Painted and polished like a new pin, she was brilliantly silhouetted by the splendid firework display that concluded a royal reception attended by HRH the Princess Royal.

After another short survey period in the Atlantic she returned to Devonport for refit.

Then over the winter of 1995/96 she went undergo routine maintenance, the major alterations being that her bow thrust doors were removed and the bow thrust tunnel was faired into the hull.

In 1996 it was decided that HMS *Herald* would be replaced by a specialist oceanographic vessel (OV) in 1999.

All in all, quite a service for the ship. Up to the time of Commander Bartholomew's booklet, published in 1996, HMS *Herald* had 13 commanders, and had steamed a total of 614,256 nautical miles.

She was put up for sale by auction in 1999 and sold in 2001, to be renamed *Somerville*. She would continue her work for three years, before being reduced to scrap metal in June 2004.

THE BUILD OF HMS *HERALD*

The following photographs show pretty well the forward end of HMS *Herald* taking shape as her bow lay in two units on the ground in front of the hull; the lower bow unit was to be erected first, followed by her upper bow unit.

HMS *Herald*, as you can imagine, brought in a lot of memories and stories from ex-crew, and from some who worked on the build of this fine ship, me included. Some of the stories are shown below:

K Eliatamby:

My father, Cdr Robert Halliday RN, was in command of HMS *Herald* in the 80s, including the Falklands War.

Above: The hull of the ship was painted in a primer called red lead – yes, it was lead-based and used everywhere in a shipyard. The superstructure on HMS *Herald* was all aluminium. Hence the different colour, as the aluminium was covered with a yellow primer.

Right: HMS *Herald* on the berth at Leith with her lower bow unit having lifting lugs welded onto it, to enable the successful lift of the 20-ton unit into position on the rest of the ship, which waits patiently – almost like a giant monster's mouth – for the rest of her hull to be completed.

Lower right: Her lower bow lifted and almost in place – but the shipbuilders of Leith were not quite good enough to land a unit with no men around. This photograph was probably taken during the tea break, or even the lunch hour, as when the men were on a work to rule there would be no working through designated breaks for any reason.

Left: HMS *Herald* complete, with her upper bow unit in place. A shipwright is landing staging on the main deck, to allow further access to the unit from outside the vessel. Two planks of timber formed each level, with a shoogly bit of scaffold for a safety rail – no hard hats or fall arresters in those days! – and the guy on the deck looks like he could be on a night out at the pub. But the reality is that the shipwrights had set all the staging up, and they really did know what they were doing, having served a proper apprenticeship in the shipyards.

Right: Her aluminium mainmast resting on keel blocks, waiting to be lifted onto her.

Above: Winter, but the build of HMS *Herald* continues.

Upper left: HMS *Herald* taking shape now, with a lot of her aluminium superstructure in place in a yellow plastic covering to protect the base metal until a primer is applied.

Left: HMS *Herald* in winter; she is tied up at the quay as outfitting continues.

Left: HMS *Herald* outfitting.

Right: A view from HMS *Herald* as she sits at her outfitting berth. Note the conditions, which were not as bad as they used to be. The ship on the stocks under construction at the top is the ferry *Pioneer*, Ship No 515 (photo by W. Russell).

John Graney:

I remember putting in the site at Cape coast when our arrival by air caused such a stir in the two nearby schools that I got a lift from a friendly local to the town police station to get some help to keep the kids back from the helicopter when landing or depositing under-slung loads. My abiding memory of taking out the site at Achowa (near Bushua Beach) by land was the Ghana Navy leading seaman/driver, walking out of the bush with a big grin on his face and a fridge balanced on his head!

Al Cole Lt RN:

I was *Herald*'s flight commander from November 1977 to July 1978. For the majority of my time with her the ship was carrying out a survey of the coast from Accra to Takoradi, and the flight's main task was to deploy and support the Decca Hi-fix sites at Cape Coast, Sharma and Achowa. Having never served with the Survey Navy before, I was somewhat surprised when early en route to Ghana uniforms were pretty much abandoned and everyone changed into what I can only describe as 'pirate rig'. Towards the very end of our deployment my Wasp (XS542) developed a tail rotor problem and was cleared for one flight only, which of course meant that all we could do was the flight back to Portland on our return. On briefing the Captain (Cdr 'Hurricane' Hearsey) about this, his response was, 'You deployed all the Hi-fix sites – you'd better work out a way to get them all back on board!' We managed this by borrowing trucks from the Ghanaian Navy, engaging native porters and carrying all the gear back to Takoradi!

Ian J. Strange:

I am trying to track down Flt Lt John Knowles, who was the pilot of HMS *Herald* Wasp helicopter. This enquiry is to do with the finding of the Argentine Skyhawk that crashed on South Jason Island in the 1982 conflict. I believe John Knowles made the discovery. Can anybody help, please?

Roberto Leandro:

I was Brazilian liaison officer of HMS *Herald* in December 1992 when the ship was in Rio de Janeiro. Her captain was Capt. Robert Alan Mark. Good ship, good crew, good times.

Mike Claydon:

I joined HMS *Herald* as engine room artificer in Leith early 1974 as part of first commission. Served through trials and service until 1977. I left as CERA soon after the *El Tambo* cattle ship fire, where as chief of the out-of-ship fire party we fought the fire – a long cold and wet night, I seem to remember. As for the infamous bow doors I spent many an hour in the flat – hammers, crowbars etc. Our conclusion: nice doors – shame about the operating equipment design. Great work with the hydrographic dept – Great ship, sad to leave her.

Dave Siggers:

I joined HMS *Herald* as its chief engine room artificer (CERA) when she was in Portsmouth dockyard for a small refit in November 1975. Whilst carrying out trials on the centre diesel generator it oversped, and the DC open coil generator disintegrated, spraying copper all round the engine room. Luckily nobody was injured, but it meant we had to run on two main generators for our workup at Portland. I was promoted to fleet chief in June 1976, and was drafted to Portland as a sea rider. A lovely ship to run as a CERA, but her water compensating stabiliser system left a lot to be desired.

Lester May Lt Cdr RN:

I was pusser of HMS *Hydra*. We sailed south with HMS *Herald* in Apr 1982, and neither ship stopped at Gibraltar. HMS *Hecla*, on the other hand, was converted to the hospital ship role in Gibraltar (the other two in Portsmouth).

Gordon Reidie:

I worked on the *Herald* as an apprentice. Lovely ship inside, although we all called them 'boats' then. I vaguely remember working in the captain's cabin, I also worked on the chart table as it was being made in the workshop. My journeyman then was Johnny Waugh.

As mentioned earlier, the next ship launched this year was the second of the boom defence ships. RMAS *Pochard* (A165), Ship No 514, launched in December 1973. She

Left: RMAS *Pochard*.
Right: *Pochard* seen from her port side.

had a longer run down the slipway than most ships launched at Leith, but took to the water as expected with no problems whatsoever.

Her specifications and dimensions were exactly the same as those of her sister ship, *Goosander*.

The Paxman History website tells us that the engines used on each of the Wild Duck class vessels were as follows: one 16RPHM for propulsion and three 6RPHZ auxiliaries.

The lofting for *Goosander* and *Pochard* was tremendously interesting for this young apprentice, with lots of wooden mock-ups of some of her more complex shapes laid out on the loft floor – all made from yellow pine, which gave off a wonderful smell as it was being worked. Strange how one remembers smells.

An interesting tale was sent into me from Iain Watt, whose father, Coagie, started his working life in the Henry Robbs yard as a heater boy, progressing to catch boy, then hudder oan (the man who held the rivet in place for the two others to hammer it in) – and finally to jointly lead the riveting squad of Watt & Broady. When riveting was eased out of the yard, he moved into the plating department. As with many in the yard, son would follow father into shipbuilding, and Iain himself had started in the yard with the ways squad. One of his abiding memories was at the launch of the boom defence vessel RMAS *Pochard*. He was tasked with being one of the men who would knock away the metal chocks just as the champagne bottle was broken over the stem of the ship.

The men who worked on the ways in the yard had to contend with all weathers – hard tough work, as they prepared the fixed ways, and the sliding ways that sat on top of the fixed ways, to allow the ship, when its full weight was held on the sliding ways, to travel down the incline into the water.

RMAS *Pochard* was built on the same ways as her sister ship *Goosander*, with the second ship much further up on the slipway and further from the water. So, on the sound of the bell, Iain would start to knock away the last of the chocks to allow the release of the daggers, then the sliding ways would move because of gravity, as the ship was on an inclined slipway. Normally the men would hammer out the chocks and make for the opening under the sliding way to get out fast from underneath. But not this time! Iain was not quick enough to make it through the aperture, and he had no option but to lie there as this great feat of engineering, weighing a few hundred tons, hurtled over the top of him. A quick visit to the toilet was required after this event, he says. Perhaps it being a cold December morning did not help, but all was good in the end, with man and ship none the worse for the experience.

While writing the above story a memory came to mind of another father and son team who worked in the yard. Crawford was the name, and for anyone who knows anything about whisky, you will know why the father was called 5 star while the son was called 3 star. The sense of humour was never far away in the shipyard.

EIGHT
ONE SHIP PER YEAR

The only ship to be launched in 1974 was the Caledonian MacBrayne car ferry MV *Pioneer*, Ship No 515.

She was being built on Berth No 3 while the outfitting of the survey ship HMS *Herald* was still being completed.

It was a poor year for the shipyard, with much aggravation between men and management alike. The outlook in the yard was not too good, and orders were few and far between, leading to a feeling of unrest, and there were always the demarcation disputes, exacerbated by an inept set of managers, one of whom thought that kicking over fires during wintertime was the way to get respect and to get the men working better.

Such acts could bring out the shipyard humour. The manager mentioned above had a human side to him; he had seen one of the older guys with boots that were almost hanging off, and arranged to get him a pair of boots. A few weeks later, the manager bumped into the proud new owner of said new boots and asked him how they were.

"Just great," was the reply, "but only one problem."

"Oh, what would that be?" replied the manager.

"Well, every time I go past a fire my leg automatically kicks out."

When orders are few and the work looks like it's soon going to run out, it is human nature to a shipbuilder to ease back a little bit – rightly or wrongly, to put the brakes on the work by whatever means possible.

And now the yard needed more orders. The work in hand would only last for so long.

It was not just in the shipyards where the mood was one of general malaise, but throughout what we would now see as the old traditional industries. The workers, in the form of the unions, were in what seemed like constant strife with government or management, or both.

With the growth of the North Sea oil boom the yard found some work in the growing ship repair/conversion business; this included work on the steel for a new terminal for the off-loading of oil at Hound Point, close to South Queensferry on the Forth.

This work, for the prime contractor, Wimpey, was good in that we got paid a higher rate for working on the walkways that would form most of the steelwork on this job. Believe me, an extra 5 pence per hour for an apprentice was very welcome then. A whole £2 per week extra made a big difference, as in those days you could still get a fair bit for £1. But prices had been rising ever since the UK had agreed to join the Common Market, as the precursor to becoming a fully paid-up member of Europe.

With wages stagnating it was not a good mix, and the inevitable strikes began.

So it was a very welcome order when it was announced that Robbs had won the tender to provide a new vessel for the ferry operator in the west of Scotland, keeping the link with the Western Isles and the mainland going.

She was to be Ship No 515 and would be named MV *Pioneer* (IMO 7341178) when she was launched in April 1974.

Her classic ferry look, with accommodation forward and vehicle deck aft, gave her an instantly recognisable look to the islanders she was to carry for some 29 years, becoming a favourite ship of so many.

Her principal dimensions as built were given as follows – length overall 67.47 metres (length B.P. 61 metres) with a moulded beam of 13.42 metres and a moulded depth of 4 metres. She was powered by two diesel oil 4SA engines, with 16 cylinders in each engine, driving her twin shafts, to produce around 3,400 bhp. Her engines were built and supplied by Mirrlees Blackstone Ltd, Stamford. She would be registered in Glasgow.

The ferry MV *Pioneer* was an order from the Scottish Transport Group, which was in effect the Caledonian MacBrayne Company but run under the auspices of the Scotland Board of Trade (or whatever it was that the politicians called themselves at that time).

The ferries were an integral way of life for the people of the Scottish Islands, who needed good reliable ships to keep their way of life and economies going. At the time, though, there always seemed to be a constant battle with government as to whether the ships were really needed.

But no matter; it was the job of the shipyard to build the ship, and to build it to the best possible standards, and so it was that this fine and well-loved ship was laid down, and the build commenced.

MV *Pioneer* is a stern/side-loading ferry built in 1974, in service for 29 years, covering nearly all of Caledonian MacBrayne's routes.

In 1978, when CalMac took over the Western Ferries terminal at Kennacraig, *Pioneer's* bridge deck was extended and her bridge wings were clipped, to help with loading.

After September 1979 she had a varied life, covering nearly all of CalMac's routes. Relief sailings for the period remained the same over the years. She also gave a winter evening, passenger-only sailing from Largs to Brodick. *Pioneer* also had brief periods at Coll, Tiree, Barra, Colonsay, Canna, Lochboisdale, Lochmaddy, Craighouse and Lochaline for passenger and livestock runs. In the summer she was emergency relief on a variety of routes.

In 1989 *Pioneer* was replaced at Mallaig by the MV *Iona* and became the spare vessel on the Upper Clyde. At this time, her hoist was removed and replaced with side ramps, allowing her to use the linkspans at Dunoon. In January 2003, after an overhaul in the James Watt dock, she took up the Mallaig and Armadale crossing, awaiting the new ship.

Left: MV *Pioneer* on sea trials in the River Forth.

Middle: The car/passenger ferry MV *Pioneer* at Eigg on her last but one day in service with CalMac, 31 October 2003 (a great photograph, taken by Graeme Phanco).

Lower: MV *Pioneer* on the Clyde, approaching Gourock Pier from Dunoon on 30 August 2003, near the end of her service with CalMac (photo by Graeme Phanco).

MV *Brenda Corlett* ex-MV *Pioneer*, Ship No 515, in West Africa
(photograph from Ian Fraser, who sailed on her in Africa).

She continued to work the Scottish Isles for a number of years before being sold to the
Corlett Group in August 2004 for work in West Africa. She would now be registered in
Gibraltar.

She was renamed *Brenda Corlett*, after the new owner's wife, and she now serves the
islands of São Tomé and Príncipe in the Gulf of Guinea, straddling the equator.

In 2006 she carried almost 300 Liberian refugees and their belongings from the Ghanaian
port of Tema to Liberia; she had been chartered to aid a repatriation effort organised by the
United Nations High Commissioner for Refugees.

The pattern was there, as now the shipyard was only managing to build and launch one
ship per year. Although ships had become much more complex this was still a poor return,
with a great many men relying on continuous orders being sourced, as in the past.

NINE
S A WOLRAAD WOLTEMADE

S A Wolraad Woltemade was for sure a sight never to be seen again in that part of Leith. Instead there now stands a shopping centre, hiding the royal yacht *Britannia* in a sort of final irony to the heritage of this part of the old town of Leith. A very popular tourist attraction, it must be said – but a vessel with absolutely no previous connection to the Port of Leith.

Lack of investment over many years had the Leith shipbuilders trying in vain to compete with other emerging shipbuilding countries, with new shipyards and tooling mostly provided

From 1976, *S A Wolraad Woltemade*, the most powerful tug in the world, fitting out after her launch. A busy shipyard scene, with a firefighting tug – Ship No 517, *Duchray* – to her stern, also fitting out. The fishery protection vessel *Scotia*, just forward of the mighty tug, is in Leith for repair (photo copyright Alan Smilie).

by the American Marshall Plan, implemented just after the Second World War, to help rebuild the shattered countries of Western Europe.

In the years to come Germany and Japan would prove to be very competitive in the shipbuilding markets, while the men at Leith were challenged to compete with them – still using, for example, rolls and flanging machines built in the late 1890s by the Carron Ironworks, the company that had supplied the cannons used in the Crimean War of the mid-1800s.

Demarcation and union involvement would, too, play their part in the demise of this great industry, not just at Leith but throughout the whole of the British Isles.

But for the time being the building of ships would continue at Leith, despite the cyclical nature and the politics involved in shipbuilding, and the yard moved on to build the mighty *S A Wolraad Woltemade*, Ship No 516 (IMO 7342873). She was an order from South African Marine Corporation Ltd (Safmarine), Cape Town, and she was to be registered in Cape Town. She would be built at Leith while her sister ship, *John Ross*, was to be built in South Africa.

(It did seem strange to me, though, that the ship named after a famous Boer hero in South Africa was to be built in Scotland, while the ship named after a famous Scottish hero was to be built in South Africa, even though he had migrated to that country.) The two ships were ordered when the Suez Canal was closed due to war in the Middle East and the bulk of the world's oil traffic was going the long way round, via the Cape of Good Hope. With that in mind, this mighty tug was also equipped to provide rescue and anti-pollution services.

S A Wolraad Woltemade would have very impressive specifications and dimensions – bigger and way more powerful than those of *Lloydsman*, the last large tug built at Leith.

This was a very welcome and large order for the yard, and even in its role as a builder of special ships she was perhaps one of the most special. Her keel was laid in April 1974.

Her dimensions on launching in May 1975 were given as follows – length B.P. 85 metres with a moulded beam of 15.2 metres and a moulded depth of 8.6 metres. She was powered by twin diesel 4SA M16-cylinder oil engines producing 19,000 bhp to her single shaft, with her propeller shrouded inside a huge Kort nozzle. Her engines were supplied and built by Mirrlees Blackstone Ltd, Stockport. At her launch her registered tonnage was given as 2,822 grt.

Her fitting out fell foul of the three-day working week, which had been introduced by the government of the day. While this of course put all the work back, the shipyard still had to contend with the terms and dates of the original contract.

But we as apprentices were not allowed to work just a three-day week. So we were there all the time – but as tradition demanded we were not allowed to do any work deemed to be that of a tradesman; this alone caused some strife, as some of the less scrupulous managers and foremen tried to get us apprentices to do tradesmen's work.

However, this was soon stopped with a few words by the union at the time.

The winter of discontent was now well upon us with the three-day week, council workers and firefighters on strike, the army called in to deal with fires, and street lights switched off for part of each week. Unsurprisingly, there was a nasty atmosphere in most of the country, certainly in the northern parts of England and in most of Scotland.

The launch of the mighty ocean salvage tug *SA Wolraad Woltemade* at Leith (origin uncertain, possibly originally shown in *Edinburgh Evening News*).

S A Wolraad Woltemade on her sea trials in the River Forth (image from own collection).

With the three-day week biting into any planned timetable of finishing the ship, it was wryly pleasing for us to hear that her sister ship was even further behind in her build in South Africa.

(This fact was conveniently forgotten by some who were involved with the ship later on.) There was even talk at the time of some men from Leith going to South Africa to help out with the build of her sister ship; over there, they had no problems with short-week working or power cuts and strikes.

This scheme, however, never materialised and after we had seen some photographs of her sister ship being built at Durban we felt it was perhaps for the better, as the conditions in the yard over there made the conditions in our yard look pretty good – which, I hasten to add, they were not. For the time they were accepted as how a working shipyard was – that is, a dangerous shit-hole if truth be told – but it was similar to most shipyards in the UK at this time.

This, I am happy to say, is now pretty much changed, most ships built under cover of huge building sheds, unlike at Leith back then, where the ships were built in the open. While the units that made up the ships were built under cover most of the time, the bow units were usually built out in the open as they tended to be larger units which the overhead cranes could not lift – so outside in all weathers it was! This did not seem to be detrimental to the quality of the build, which I would say was more to do with the skill of the experienced shipbuilders at the time. They could have built the ships anywhere.

And get built she did, despite the circumstances; the men from Leith could indeed be proud of producing the finest ocean-going tug afloat.

It would take a whole volume to do justice to this amazing ship, the *grande dame* of all ocean-going salvage tugs.

Sure, there are more powerful tugs around the world today, but they don't look anything as good as the *Wolraad Woltemade*.

She looked the part – fine lines allied with a very powerful aura. She was a real greyhound of the seas – or, depending on your viewpoint, a formidable vulture lurking off the coast of South Africa, scanning the world's radio waves for that distress call to come in. Then she would take off with all of her more than 26,000 hp, racing through some of the worst seas imaginable to claim her very valuable prize.

But back to her build. As mentioned earlier she was very impressive even on the slipway, and she was completed with a magnificent bit of work that formed her huge bulbous bow.

Fitting out – looking down on her after deck with the small firefighting tug *Duchray,* Ship No 517, at her stern (image, own collection).

S A Wolraad Woltemade arrives at Cape Town after her maiden voyage (photo copyright David Shackleton, and shown here by permission).

One of her pair of Mirrlees KV 16-cylinder (9,600 hp) engines being lifted into her by a mobile crane capable of a 100-ton lift. The shipyard cranes could not lift this heavy engine as it was above their lifting capacity. The engine would be eased into position using sliding ways, just as when a ship was launched. The two ways are on the left of this photograph, with a man standing on each one.

This was first done as a mock-up in the loft, then the plater lifted a metal cage of the mock-up and, along with some heating from the blacksmiths, they produced what I would call a real bulbous bow.

Some of the figures for this ship were very impressive for her day, such as her 210-ton bollard pull, with her single screw variable pitch propeller set inside a fixed Kort nozzle geared to her two massive 16-cylinder Mirrlees engines.

S A Wolraad Woltemade was capable of racing along at more than 21 knots. With her twin rudders fitted at the after end of her nozzle, she had a turning circle *at full speed* of around two ship's lengths, and she could also stop dead in the water in just under one minute in just over one and a half ship's lengths – and she was just 5 metres short of 100 metres overall length. Her twin rudders aft of her Kort nozzle along with her powerful bow thruster unit gave her a lot of manoeuvrability for a large ship.

A note about the Kort nozzles from Wikipedia:

A **ducted propeller**, also known as a **Kort nozzle**, is a marine propeller fitted with a non-rotating nozzle. It is used to improve the efficiency of the propeller and is especially used on heavily loaded propellers or propellers with limited diameter. It was developed first by Luigi Stipa (1931) and later by Ludwig Kort (1934). The Kort nozzle is a shrouded propeller assembly for marine propulsion. The cross-section of the shroud has the form of a foil, and the shroud can offer hydrodynamic advantages over bare propellers, under certain conditions.

Robert Rowbottom told me an interesting story about the concerns that the yard had at the time of her launch. Both he, as the naval architect, and the management were worried that the huge ship might hit the sill of the dock gates when they were lifted, just before the vessel achieved buoyancy.

So the shipwright gaffer, Bobby Aitchison, and one of the managers came up with the idea of filling up all available space at her stern with empty oil drums. Her large Kort nozzle was boarded up and filled with oil drums to aid buoyancy.

This puzzled many people at her launch, the story told that it was a shroud as her steering and power arrangement were a secret. But now you know it was just to aid her buoyancy as she went into the water, and needless to say she had no such problems on her launch, taking to the water like a swan.

The mighty *S A Wolraad Woltemade* was launched into the waters of the Leith Dock Basin in May 1975. She was so powerful that she could not do her bollard pull trials in Leith, and

Left: In dry dock in Singapore, and a nice perspective of her size (photo, Kit Cooper).

Lower: Again, in dry dock in Singapore. This photograph gives some idea of the size of the Kort nozzle on *Wolraad Woltemade*; she had dropped the *S A* from her name by the time the picture was taken (photo, Kit Cooper).

she had to sail around the coast of Scotland to do them on the Clyde near Greenock, another home of Scottish shipbuilding excellence. After her successful trials she was handed over to her proud owners at Safmarine in April 1976. With her call sign, ZTUG, painted on her superstructure side, she just looked right.

Her build had not been without some difficulty but as she sailed out of Leith there were many proud shipbuilders almost with a tear in the eye.

And right she was, as she took up her station on the coast of South Africa, ever alert for a supertanker to find itself in trouble in this stormy part of the world.

With a crew of around 42 she was capable of staying on station at sea for quite some time, and she was well equipped for almost any type of emergency; she had firefighting gear, including two water cannons capable of firing over 600 tons of water per hour. And she even had a four-berth sick bay for emergency medical cases.

She had a separate winch house just aft of the bridge to control her two huge friction winches, with static loads of 320T and 180T, and with their spooling winches holding more than 2,000 metres of 70 mm and 56 mm diameter wire towing hawsers. This ship could tow anything afloat at the time, and more.

Above: Bringing a huge tanker into Cape Town after another tow in 1982 (photo, Bob Terry).

Left: Now *that's* what you call a turbocharger, undergoing repair Everything on this supertug was large (photo, Kit Cooper).

Wolraad Woltemade arriving at Cape Town, passing the container terminal 1982 (photo, Bob Terry).

The following photos were supplied to me by Kit Cooper, the second engineer on the mighty tug, when she was involved with the refloat of the huge tanker *Front Rider*, stuck on sandbanks in Singapore.

She was also employed in taking oil rigs from the builders' yards, by that time primarily located in Asia, as most of the building work had moved to the east, just as shipbuilding had before – more money to be made from the lower labour costs.

Left: *Front Rider* stuck fast, as the mighty *Wolraad Woltemade* moves in astern to get a line on her.

Middle: 102 Not long now, as the mighty tug takes charge.

Lower left: Moving in to take *Front Rider* in tow …

Lower right: *Front Rider* now safely under tow by *Wolraad Woltemade*; all in a day's work for the tug.

Thanks to Kit Cooper, we can follow the tow of one of those huge oil rigs from the builder's yard to delivery at an oilfield:

Above: Looking aft from the winch control room

Left: Towing the oil rig *Orlan* from South Korea just after the rig had been built.

Right: A nice night-time shot of the oil rig under tow.

Left: Another successful delivery for *Wolraad Woltemade*.

Right: *Wolraad Woltemade* in Singapore in 1994, without her large after A-frame mast, which had been removed due to some stability concerns. Still a great-looking ship, but not quite as she had been built (photo from Stephen Carson, second engineer).

Politics would interfere with decisions taken about the two sister ships. *Wolraad Wolte-made* had some problems with her crankshaft; when cracking was discovered the irrational decision was taken to send her to the scrapyard, while the local-built – and, to many from the northern hemisphere, inferior – ship was to be kept. A sad day for all involved with the *Wolraad Woltemade*. I have since been told that one of the crazy repairs that had been carried out on the ship had involved taking a shaft from a land-based power station and using this in her. Such a move would or could have created the oscillations, slight at first, that may well have contributed to the cracks to be found later in her starboard crankshaft. Who knows? Land-based materials are not usually compatible with marine engines.

View from the pilot boat leaving the huge tug (image, Kit Cooper).

She was one of the ships built at Leith that generated the most correspondence to me, some of which are featured here:

Peter Young:

If you look at the last picture before of the *Wolraad* while she was still whole, you will see that the call sign was ZFFA and not ZTUG. WW and sister JR were first registered in South Africa with ZTUG and ZTOW. Because of sanctions during the apartheid era, they were re-registered with ZFFA and ZCLT call signs in Hamilton, Bermuda (which, according to my seaman's record book, must have been before 1980). In April 1982 the Falklands War broke out. To avoid being requisitioned by the British Navy for use in the war (Bermuda being a British colony), on 18 April 1982 I signed off the *Wolraad Woltemade*, ZFFA and then signed on again on the *Wolraad Woltemade* ZTUG. Later the tugs were re-registered in Panama. This explains the various colour changes of the ships' funnels.

I sailed on the WW and John Ross as electrician between 1979 and 1983.

Some of the crew I remember well are: Richard Armstrong (4th to chief engineer), Eddie Freestone CE, Eugene Hermanus (3rd Eng) Walter Du Preez, (4th–-3rd Eng), Nic Carrington (CE), Jimmy Hey (2nd–CE) Adrian Bonello (2nd Eng), Peter Stow (mate) Simon Atherstone-Reynolds (2nd mate), Dave Stirling (3rd mate), Terry Purden (mate), and the five captains: Steve Mathews, Robin Jones, Danny Betts, Jack Golden, and even Frank (chicken coop) Colbard. I sailed with all of them, and I have far more happy memories than otherwise. There must be many more – but I, like the tugs, am getting old.

Wolraad Woltemade and *John Ross*,

I salute you and all who sailed in you!

Dave Moir:

I had the honour of being towed by the *John Ross* on the oil rig, the *Chris Chenery* from UK North Sea to dry dock in Rotterdam. The tow went so well, very professionally done, *John Ross's* skipper was the towmaster. We were overloaded on the rig at start of tow due to fog preventing helicopters, so some of the rig crew sailed on the *John Ross*. I sailed on the rig, did customs forms for the bargemaster and watched the tug as she towed us effortlessly to R'dam. When she cast off she blew her horn, which blasted right round the whole of the Europoort!

Mark De Simone:

I had the great fortune to know both the *Wolraad Woltemade* and the *John Ross*, first encountering the *WW* in HKUD during 1984 or 85, while my own vessel, Sedco 600, was stacked. I had the great honour of being a guest aboard the *WW*, meeting Captain

Jack and his amazing crew. Then later in Houston, during 1985, I met up with the *John Ross*, and then in 1986, in Singapore on a stopover while the *WW* was towing the *Zane Barnes* from Nagoya to the Gulf of Mexico.

The images of these amazing vessels remain with me today, and as I learned on the *WW* in HKUD, while on board one cannot use the 'PIG', refer to the vessel as a 'boat' or proceed in conversation more than 5 minutes without mentioning women … it was a great experience and I am proud to have known these vessels and their personnel. It was a bit of a shock to see the *WW* split in half at the end of the article, but I suppose after nearly 40 years' service, it is to be expected … and life goes on. May it rest in peace!

Tim Callais:

The photo of *WW* towing that yellow-hulled rig was taken around March or April 1993. The rig was the *Transocean Richardson*, and I was on it at the time the picture was taken. We were en route to the Gulf of Mexico from Scotland. She was a beautiful tug and made for an excellent journey in her wheel wash.

Stephen Ward:

I remember reading in the *Guinness Book of Records* how the *Wolraad Woltemade* was the world's most powerful tug of her day. She was indeed very special.

Ken Hunter:

Having being the senior service engineer for Mirrlees Blackstone, I was the engineer responsible for installations of *WW* and *JR*'s engine/propulsion systems, and carried out both ships' start-ups at builders, both basin trials, sea trials/bollard pull trials (*WW*) and the maiden trips of both. I have fabulous memories of these amazing ladies, and love reading about them and revisiting my halcyon days.

TEN
BRITISH SHIPBUILDERS

Not long after the order for the huge tug had come in, the yard won a contract to build another three harbour/firefighting tugs for use in and around the North Sea, to support the oil industry. These three ships would continue the long tradition of building tugs at the Leith Shipyards.

Ship No 517 was one of three such tugs ordered to be built at Leith, and a welcome order it was. The other two tugs were for the Grangemouth & Forth Towing Co., and were built for operation in the Forth at the Hound Point oil terminal, which was also built at the Leith Shipyards.

Duchray, Ship No 517, in the Western Basin at Leith (image from own collection).

Ship No 517's keel was laid in November 1974, and she, the first of the three-ship order, was to be launched in June 1975. She would take the name *Duchray* (IMO 7392816). She and her sister ship, *Boquhan*, Ship No 518, were built on the same slipway, with the *Duchray* ahead of her sister ship.

Duchray's specifications and dimensions were given as follows – length overall 38.16 metres (length B.P. 34 metres) with a moulded beam of 9.2 metres and a moulded depth of 4.5 metres. She was powered by a 4SA V12 cylinder Ruston/Paxman type 12RKCM, connected to a controllable propeller; producing around 2,640 bhp, to her single shaft giving her a service speed of 14 knots. Her engine was built and supplied by Ruston Paxman Diesels Ltd, Newton-le-Willows. She had a bollard pull of 38 tons. Her registered tonnage at launch was given as 328 grt, and she would be registered at Grangemouth.

Ship No 518 was the harbour tug *Boquhan* (IMO 7392828) launched in August 1975 and completed in January 1976. She was the sister ship to *Duchray*, with the exact same specs and dimensions, including a very distinctive mast arrangement, with three powerful water cannons on it. *Duchray* and *Boquhan* were a common sight in the Forth, shepherding the large oil tankers to the Hound Point terminal, to discharge their loads of crude oil.

In 1998 *Duchray* was sold by Grangemouth & Forth Towing to the Norwegian company Eide Marine Services A/S – Bergen, and renamed *Eide Rex*. At the time of writing she is still operating there under that name – with some additions, as you can see in the photograph, but still essentially the same ship.

Flying Childers, Ship No 519 (IMO 7392830), was the final tug from the three-ship order. She was slightly different in that she was an order for the Clyde Shipping Company, and her mast did not go up to full height, she having no requirement for the firefighting equipment; it has to be said that she did not really look complete without the full height of her mast. But apart from the change to her mast she had the exact same specs and dimensions as the other two tugs. She was launched from the yard in December 1975.

Left: *Duchray* as *Eide Rex*, seen in the River Tyne in 2005. She was on her way to pick up a barge (photo Kevin Blair, with permission).

Right: *Duchray* nearest, with her sister ship *Boquhan* passing in the Forth.

76

Above: HMS *Brazen*, a Type 22 frigate, heading into Glasgow in 1983 for a weekend visit, with *Flying Childers* in attendance (photo, Paul Strathdee).

Right: The bulk carrier MV *Garrison Point* at Leith, fitting out in 1978 (image from own collection).

She worked on the Clyde for almost 20 years, making her one of the oldest tugs working on the river, well liked and a very familiar sight on the river, until 1995 when she ran into rocks in the Kyle of Lochalsh and was grounded. She was laid up in Greenock for a few years after this mishap, and she just lay at her berth wasting away before finally being sold for scrap around 2001/2002 when she was lifted from the water and transported to Padstow, in Cornwall, for scrapping in 2002.

The bulk cargo carrier *Garrison Point*, Ship No 520 (IMO 7400924), a very welcome order, was one of the largest ships built and launched at the Leith Shipyards of Henry Robb. At just over 8,000 gross tonnes and with a length in excess of 120 metres (370 feet) she had a lot of steelwork in her, and I remember that she had more bloody beam knees than any other ship I ever worked on. (One of the jobs in the loft given to apprentices or young journeymen was to lift all the beam knees from the full-size lines and create a paper template for each one of them – and she had hundreds of them.) She was launched from the yard in 1977.

Her dimensions at launching in August 1976 were given as follows – length overall 128.02 metres (length B.P. 120 metres), with a moulded beam of 19.5 metres and a moulded depth of 11.5 metres. She was powered by a diesel oil 4SA 12-cylinder Pielstick engine producing around 6,000 bhp to her single shaft. Her engine was built and supplied by Crossley Premier Engineering Co. Ltd, Manchester. Her registered tonnage at her launch in August 1976 was given as 8,014 grt. She would be registered in the Port of London.

She had been ordered by the Thornhope Shipping Co. Ltd., and was to be managed by the Hudson Steamship Company Ltd.

She would be chartered out to the Central Electricity Generating Board, and used to supply power stations with coal – a real tale of bringing coals from Newcastle, where she used to load on the Tyne for deliveries in the south of England.

Above: LPG/C *Borthwick*, built in 1976 for George Gibson & Co. Ltd. This picture was taken off *Teesport* 1988 (photo by her master, David Reid, with permission).

Left: The tanker *Borthwick* running her sea trials in the River Forth (image from own collection).

MV *Claymore* was another ferry on the stocks, ordered by Caledonian MacBrayne, who must have been very pleased with MV *Pioneer*, the previous ship they had ordered from Robbs.

In 1988 she was renamed to run under the Bahamas flag, before being sold on to Stephenson Clarke in 1989 and renamed again, as *Jevington*, still under the flag of the Bahamas. (Not to be confused with another ship built at the Leith Shipyards of Henry Robb that was also renamed *Jevington*; this was the MV *Macaulay*, Ship No 468.)

She was to end up being scrapped in Spain in April 2000, so she had a relatively short sea career of only 23 years.)

The next ship on the stocks at Robbs was an order from the shipping company George Gibson Ltd, one of the many based in Leith at the time. It's just a pity that more of the local shipping companies did not order ships from the shipyard just across the road, so to speak.

It was a very welcome order, just the same, and it was for a ship to carry liquid gas, so she was of a pretty special design and construction. *Borthwick*, Ship No 521 (IMO 7604867), was launched in March 1977.

I seem to remember that she had three huge gas tanks fitted into her hull. They were made by a specialised outside contractor, and arrived at the shipyard to be fitted into the hull as she was being built.

I remember, too, that the yard had a lot of trouble as the owners were constantly making design changes, and changes to her wing tanks in particular.

She was named, as most of the Gibson ships were, after names and characters in the Walter Scott novels. He had visited, and been most impressed by, Borthwick, a castle in the Scottish Borders not far from Edinburgh, where Mary Queen of Scots had stayed shortly after marrying Bothwell.

(And no, she was *not* named after shipwright Stevie of the same surname, forever mumping his gums about us building a ship named after him!)

She was owned and operated by George Gibson Tankers from her launch till she was sold in 1991, when she operated in the Unigas Consortium.

She was then sold on to Peruvian owners to continue plying her trade with cargoes of butadiene in South American waters, until sold for scrap in 2010 and being run onto the beach at Alang, along with so many other ships, to be broken up.

The MV *Claymore* was the third CalMac ship of that name. She was a half-sister to the *Pioneer*, although somewhat larger and able to carry more passengers. She was used on the run from Oban to the outer isles of Scotland's west and rugged coast, where she was a well-known sight and a well-loved ship for more than ten years.

With her four passenger decks, complete with saloons and bars, and cabins for 32 people, she could carry around 500 people with ease, and with 50 cars on her after vehicle deck she was an impressive ship.

She was also chartered to Hamilton Oil, and ran out of ports in Wales. Along with being the summer relief ship for CalMac she was used as a ferry to take passengers down the Clyde. Her 'Doon the Water' trips were popular with the residents of Glasgow, and she was used for the annual Govan Shipbuilders' trips doon the water as well.

MV *Claymore* was perhaps the most travelled of all the CalMac ferries, having also been used to ferry passengers to Douglas, Isle of Man, during 1994 to 1996, for which she was given an international passenger certificate for 300.

For three years *Claymore* operated a new summer sailing from Campbeltown to Ballycastle in Northern Ireland, but this run was found to be unprofitable so after a five-week charter to the Faroe Islands in 2000, she was moved to Birkenhead and put up for sale.

She was bought by Pentland Ferries; as she was a very good seakeeping ship she was ideal as a relief ferry on the stormy passage from the Scottish mainland over the Pentland Firth to Orkney, a role she undertook from 2002 until 2006, when her

In May 1997 *Claymore* was sold to Argyll and Antrim Steam Packet Company, a subsidiary of Sea Containers Scotland Ltd (image by Jack Molls).

role changed somewhat, and she was used on a short-term charter to carry livestock from Dover to Calais.

In 2009 she was sold on to CT Offshore, and her new owners, christening her *Sia*, and planning to use her as a cable layer, added four forward bow thrusters to her hull along with three aft thrusters. This was to give her a dynamic positioning capability for her new role, and at the time of writing she is believed to still be working for the Danish company.

An interesting working life for another fine ship from Robbs.

As we reached the end of the 1970s, it was a time of great political upheaval and a distinct lack of shipbuilding orders. However, Robbs managed to secure some work by much good fortune – but sadly at the expense of another shipyard, a small one in Wales, which was then forced to close down.

This was an order from the Paal Wilson Shipping Company for a mini-bulk carrier, MV *Rhino*.

The whole job was a bit strange, as Robbs was only contracted to do the steelwork. This meant that the ship would be built and launched as a hull with no superstructure – that was to be fitted in Norway by the owners.

Her ship's lines had already been done – and this too was a first, as her lines had been done by computer to an existing design, and had been run out full size in the body plan on a plastic stable film, which meant that there was no requirement for a scrieve board (a sign of the times to come …).

The job of building the bare hull of the MV *Rhino* was, as ever, taken on and completed despite all the turmoil going on in the country and the fear of unemployment just around the corner – or, in the case of a shipyard, when the last order was completed.

MV *Rhino*, Ship No 523 (IMO 7616860), was launched in April 1978. This hull was then completed by Georg Eide e Sonner AS., Høylandsbygd, Norway (Yard No.109). Her given dimensions were as follows – length B.P. 66 metres with a moulded beam of 13.4 metres and a moulded depth of 6.5 metres. Her completed registered tonnage was given as 1,445 grt.

Once finished she was towed over to Bergen, Norway, to be completed.

This ship was another vessel which was to undergo a conversion, to make her almost 20 metres longer overall in 1983. Her registered tonnage increased to 2,169 grt. The MV *Rhino* was broken up in 2009, so she had a working span of around 30 years, which is not bad for her owners.

And then there were empty slipways at Robbs. With no orders in the books things did not look too promising for the yard.

If a government is intent on destroying an industry – any industry – then first it has to have control over that industry, and during the nasty 1970s plans were moving in that direction. In 1977, under the provisions of the Aircraft and Shipbuilding Industries Act of that year, the yard became part of the nationalised British Shipbuilders, which had been formed by the government to try and streamline and improve the competitiveness of the British yards. This amalgamation was part of the Geddes Axe, the recommendation of Sir Eric Geddes, which destroyed the railway network in the United Kingdom – a network that they are only now trying to revive, in some areas.

Times were starting to get very tough in the shipbuilding industry in the UK; the government of the day was clearly against all the traditional industries which the British Isles had been built on. If you worked in the steel industry or as a coal miner or shipbuilder (all union shops) it was apparent that you were the enemy of the day as far as the government was concerned. This was the start of a so-called new revolution in the industrial world of the UK, and one we are still paying for today, as the country was turned into a service and financial base for other people's money.

This was the time when British Shipbuilders should have been investing capital and time into the Leith shipyard; with more modern plant and a covered building berth, the future could have been very different for the yard.

But lack of investment in the UK, along with a lack of interest or understanding of this industry, had the other shipbuilding countries smiling and moving ahead of our antiquated shipyards.

Now Robbs' yard, with little or no work around, was running a skeleton staff. But then an order was announced by British Shipbuilders: two motor crane barges for use in the Polish port of Zarzad Portu in Szczecin. That was the total order for the Leith Shipyards from a 50-ship order, which tells you that at the time the consortium had no real interest in the smaller shipyards of the British Isles; they were only interested in the larger centres – which of course had many more workers, and therefore a larger voter base to try and manipulate.

While it was a welcome order at the time, after the yard had been virtually empty for six months or so, and many had lost their jobs, it was a pittance from a government that obviously did not care – nor, as it transpired, had any real clue how to run a group dedicated to commercial shipbuilding.

The two barges were built at the same time, and although they consisted of a fair amount of steelwork there was little outfitting in them, so once again the uncertainty of the future hung over everyone who worked in the yard at the time.

It was not a good time to be working there, but at least it was a job, when all around the country jobs were being shed in most of the manufacturing industries.

The first crane barge was not named but given a number: DP-ZPS-6. The barges were just large rectangular boxes with a crane on top. Their dimensions were identical: 36.6 metres in length by 18.5 metres in breadth with a depth of 3.66 metres. Tonnage was given as 290 grt. They were both built on the same berth, and the first one launched in February 1979. The sister, Ship No 525, was named DP-ZPS-7 and launched in May 1979. As far as I am aware they are still operating in Poland to this day.

Halfway through this order I decided to move on from the shipyard; it was no fun working there any more, with the constant hassle and threat of being laid off. I planned to leave shipbuilding, and did so for a while, before being tempted back to work on the lofting for what would be the last two ships built at Leith.

ELEVEN
INTO THE 80s

The next order was another very welcome one: two more tugs very similar to some previous ones built at Robbs.

The order was from the Nigerian Port Authority, and the two harbour tugs were near-sister ships of the *Flying Childers*, built a couple of years earlier, in that they had the same specifications and size as the *Flying Childers*, though they would be twin screw rather than single. They would be powered by two 6-cylinder 4SA diesel engines driving two shafts. The engines were built and supplied by Mirrlees Blackstone (Stamford) Ltd. Their registered tonnage was given as 326 grt.

Nice-sized harbour tugs and very versatile, they would work well and last for many years.

Bajima, Ship No 526 (IMO 7820447), was the first to be built, and was launched in the first months of the new decade. (If you wonder what it was like in Scotland around this time, I would suggest you read one of Irvine Welsh's books, to give you a decent insight into life in parts of Edinburgh and Leith during the first half of the decade.)

The *Bajima* was delivered to Nigeria – and, as ever with ships that end up there, not much is known about what become of her. From 1997 her owners were registered as 'unknown', and she was last heard of in 2009.

Left: *Bajima* fitting out at Leith 1980 (photo, Paul Fairfield).

Right: *Burutu* fitting out at Leith, 1980; you can just see the stern of her sister ship, *Bajima*, forward of her bows (photo, Paul Fairfield).

Ship No 527 was the second of the two-ship order from Nigeria. She was named *Burutu* (IMO 7820459), of the same spec and size as *Bajima*. She was launched in May 1980.

After the *Burutu* was delivered to Nigeria her records too were lost – although, as you will see from the photograph, she appears to have been run onto a mudbank and left to rot there.

She was the last of a fine pedigree of tugs built at Robbs.

It turned out that a tug was built and launched for every year of the shipyard's working lifetime.

A grand total of 66 tugs were built to the highest standards at the shipyard, from small ones to the world's largest and most powerful at the time; and all through the dark days of the Second World War tugs were continually produced.

After I left, things started to look up for the yard, and for a while there was a new mood of optimism in the place, so I was told. Shipbuilders have to be supreme optimists, as there is forever the thought that without a constant stream of orders coming into the shipyard the better and faster you produce, the sooner you will be out of a job.

A sad end for a fine vessel. The *Burutu* stuck on a mudbank on some river in Nigeria; she was the last in a long line of well-built tugs from the Leith

The dredger *Mersey Mariner* doing what she was built for.

The next order received by Robbs was for a dredger, *Mersey Mariner*. She was aptly named, as she would be working to keep that great waterway leading into the port of Liverpool free of silt and mud to allow all the great ships that visited the famous old port enough clearance to navigate the river without fear of grounding.

The *Mersey Mariner* was a fair-sized ship for a dredger, and would provide work at Robbs for a year or so.

She was launched into the waters of Leith Docks in 1981, and after fitting-out she was delivered to her new owners for work on the Mersey, where she was a well-known sight for many years to come with her distinctive three grab cranes on her deck. It was only a couple of years ago that she was eventually sold to a Brazilian concern to work on the other side of the Atlantic, where at the time of writing she is still working, just in warmer waters.

TWELVE
THV *PATRICIA*

The next ship on the stocks was the twin-screw THV *Patricia*, Ship No 530, at 2,639 grt. She was launched on 30 September 1981.

She was officially designated as a buoy/lighthouse tender. She had been ordered by Trinity House, the ancient authority responsible for the upkeep and maintenance of all the safety devices around the coasts of England and Wales. The institution also, of course, looks after the men and ships that sail around the coast and rely on lighthouses and buoys to help them navigate safely. Scotland has her own equivalent in the Northern Light House Commission.

THV *Patricia* was a fair-size ship, and the order was very welcome at the yard during tough times for shipbuilders in the United Kingdom. She was built to the highest standards and more – never have I seen carpets with such a thick pile on them and, along with gold-plated taps for the water runs, she was a real ship of luxury for the time, considering that she is in fact a hard-working ship doing a tough job at sea. Her teak decks were a credit to the shipwrights of the Leith yard; they seemed to invite bare feet to walk over them.

The story we heard at the time was that her outfitting had been done to such a high standard because of the strong possibility that she was going to stand in for the Royal Yacht *Britannia*; there was a lot of speculation as to what was going to happen to the Queen's own ship.

THE BUILD OF THV *PATRICIA*

The following photographs record some of the build of THV *Patricia*, and my thanks go to Charlie the welder for my being able to show this record of her build.

Above: THV *Patricia* on the far berth,
with her upper bow unit in place.

Right: THV *Patricia* with the upper bow unit in place.

Above: THV *Patricia*, looking down from the bridge and
onto her bow with the Black Shed in the background.

Right: THV *Patricia* ready to launch.

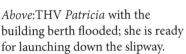

Above:THV *Patricia* with the building berth flooded; she is ready for launching down the slipway.

Upper right: THV *Patricia* begins to gather pace after the shipwrights have released the daggers.

Right: THV *Patricia* at the point of no return – always a time when something could go wrong, as she passes over the sill of the dock just before buoyancy occurs.

Lower right: THV *Patricia* safely launched, with her tug now looking after her; note all the debris from her sliding ways, all this has to be brought back to shore by the shipwrights.

Left: After the launch of THV *Patricia* the work is not over for the shipwrights. While the launch party goes off for drinks and canapés the men work to drag the sliding ways back to shore. Smaller debris would be collected by rowing boat, and only then will the shipwrights be able to take some time out and perhaps decide, as tradition demands, where they will spend the launch monies shared between them.

Below: The Trinity House Vessel *Patricia* on her way out to sea trials in the Firth of Forth (Barry Booth Collection).

Lower: The magnificent wooden after deck on THV *Patricia*; note the small cradle to take the signal cannon on the aft starboard side of the deck (Barry Booth Collection).

THV *Patricia* fitting out at Leith (Barry Booth collection).

The Trinity House Vessel *Patricia* is still working away around the coasts of England, Wales and the Channel Islands, and such is the level of accommodation on her that the ship also offers cruises for up to 12 passengers, who can join her at one of her many ports and cruise around while the ship carries out her many duties.

As the flagship of Trinity House she also carries out a lot of official functions, so she is a busy ship, and we hope she will continue as such for a few years to come.

While I never personally worked on this ship, she was fitting out in the basin when I returned to the yard – or she may have been back for her first-year maintenance period, which would seem more likely.

I shall leave the last words about this ship to Robert Rowbottom, the naval architect at the Leith yard:

THV *Patricia* edging away from the quayside on the way to do more sea trials (Barry Booth collection).

Ship No 530, *Patricia*

I saw [a mention of *Patricia*] in a magazine for pensioners last year. They're now promoting her as a luxury short trip cruise ship … 6 cabins and a few guests round the English and Welsh coastlines.

I thought it somewhat ironic as this was the ship that sank us in Leith. She was fitted out to a standard far above her station in service. Of course they told us the royal family would use her when the *Britannia* was unavailable.

THV *Patricia* (photo, Reg. Mordecai).

The big goalpost masts were said to be somewhat ugly, but they were functional. She was half yacht, half light house tender. The speed crane derricks could handle a 20-ton lift. … Somewhat tender in certain conditions but fast transfer ballast tanks took care of any excessive heeling.

The consultants were Three Quays, a P&O subsidiary.

I remember they laughed when we told them her lines were based on Ship No 379, *Mombasa*, launched in 1949 at Leith. We had the last laugh when she achieved her design speed easily on the measured mile – but we lost a lot of money on this contract.

End of story!

No doubt about it, the THV *Patricia* is a fine-looking ship, and elicits memories from those who worked on her and who still do work on her:

Graeme McCormack:

THV *Patricia*: as the keel was in part-assembly sections, the first of the fitting trades started putting fuel lines in. Something in me now says they were 3". This size is rare on land work. The first lengths were into the double bottoms. The fitters were John Whitecross, John [Jock] Gold, fitter's mate Peter Johnston and myself, Graeme McCormack, apprentice, aka junior.

Tim Leggett:

I used to be a seaman in THV *Patricia* as well as being second steward in RRS *Bransfield*, both built by Robb Caledon. The first master of *Bransfield* was a Tommy Woodman who went on to be an Elder Brother of Trinity House. He was instrumental in the building of both these ships, and he told me that when they designed *Patricia* they took the plans of *Bransfield* as a starting point, as they needed a similar size ship as a supply and working ship as well as partially a passenger ship. Although a lot different, as they were built for different purposes and years apart, I think the likeness shows. I loved working aboard both these ships.

Richard Woodman:

Tim Leggett is not quite correct. The name he wants is Tom Woodfield. I served in the ship as captain, and having the name Woodman probably caused the confusion. But yes indeed, I went on to be an Elder Brother of Trinity House. *Patricia* is a fine ship and was a delight to handle. She was very well able to cope with extreme weather, and her practical ability as a multifunctional tender is impressive. I was very sad when I left her to swallow the anchor, always having an excellent ship's company.

THIRTEEN
THE STRUGGLE TO STAY OPEN

At the start of the 1980s not all was gloom as far as shipbuilding was concerned, as we had the panacea of North Sea oil, discovered in the previous decade. The oil was beginning to flow now, and with every new oilfield there was the need for new ships to service and supply all the oil rigs that were formed in the British sector of the North Sea.

But what should have been even more boom times for shipyards in Scotland in particular turned out to be considerably less than once believed.

As mentioned earlier, the government of the day had closed down the Dundee yard, and the Leith Shipyards of Robb Caledon had reverted to its original name, Henry Robb Ltd. And now, with the Dundee (Caledon) yard closed down, this left only two other yards in Scotland which could claim to be the right size for building oil rig supply vessels; one of these was Hall Russell in Aberdeen, and the other was Ferguson's yard on the lower Clyde.

The shipyard at Leith had three building berths, so it could build a minimum of three ships per year. And the oilfields needed ships by the hundred, so even with a ten-year plan in place the yard could have built around 30 ships for them.

But it seems that for whatever reason this was another golden opportunity for continued long employment for Robbs that was wasted by British Shipbuilders. As things turned out the Leith yard built only two.

The *Seaforth Sovereign* was the first of the rig supply ships to be built at Robbs; her design was based on a tried and tested concept for such ships. She was a bog-standard twin-screw rig supply ship, and she should have been the first of many such ships to be built at the yard.

She had been ordered by the Seaforth Maritime Company, and she continued to work for Seaforth until it sold its North Sea ships to the Norwegian Shipping Company Farstad – which thus became the largest operator of rig supply ships in the North Sea. In 2003 *Seaforth Sovereign* was sold on to United Arab shipping interests and, renamed *Sis Champ*, was converted to a standby safety/supply ship.

(As an aside, it was either the *Seaforth Sovereign* or Robbs' next rig supply ship, *Balder Leith*, which appeared in one of the James Bond films.)

Left: *Seaforth Sovereign* heading out to do her sea trials in the Firth of Forth (Barry Booth Collection).

Middle: 150 *Seaforth Sovereign* heading out to sea trials (Barry Booth collection).

Lower: Ex-*Seaforth Sovereign* now *Far Sky* refitting at the A&P ship repair yard at Wallsend, on the Tyne, 10 May 2002. Docks and yard now closed, and work transferred to the large dry dock at the former Palmers Shipyard at Hebburn on the River Tyne (photo, Reg Mordecai).

This print, sent to me by R. Rowbottom, shows the *Balder Leith* on sea trials.

The oil rig supply ship *Balder Leith* was the second rig supply ship. She was a design by the Norwegian Ulstein Group, which has gone on from strength to strength, and again, if the yard at Leith had been able to capitalise on this market then they could have made big inroads on the path of modernisation; most of the rig supply ships were basically the same, so modern production methods could have been introduced instead of, as up until that time, each new ship being a totally new job of work.

The use of permanent and semi-permanent jigs and fixtures would have increased production and accuracy dramatically.

Balder Leith was built partly by a shipyard on the Tyne which shall remain nameless. It was responsible for building her stern unit and part of the bow, and the welded seams at the stern are as bad a job as I have ever seen. While all yards were under British Shipbuilders, they still had to fight for orders – orders which were scarce at the time, so one might even be tempted to say that a competing yard would not wish to produce work of a good standard in the hope that the receiving yard would then have major problems. British Shipbuilders had yards competing against one another rather than acting in concert; they left the yards to fight over scraps like seagulls for food.

In addition, not all was going great in the old yard by this time, and the attending super was not too impressed with some of the work that arrived from the Tyne. The Leith yard was not exempt from criticism either, as a lot of experience had by now gone from the yard. The quality of build, both the steelwork and the outfitting, was not as good as it used to be.

Some of the electrical and plumbing work was done at Leith, where by this time the yard was using sub-contracted workers in the effort to be more productive. Yet another great idea that had come out of British Shipbuilders – fill the place with people who don't know one end of a ship from another and still expect the same quality of workmanship. A plumber could, they apparently thought, come into the shipyard from outside and do the same work; it seems they never wondered why the old trades had the prefix 'ship's' before them, as in ship's plumber, ship's carpenter and so on. Those specialists had been trained in building ships, not houses.

At the time of writing she is owned by Italian shipping interests and working as an offshore tug/supply ship specialising in anti-oil pollution and converted accordingly. She is on contract

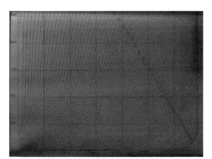

Left: Part of the fore body lines of Ship No 532 done on CAD, and a sign of times to come (image from own collection).

Below: *Balder Leith*'s aft end on the slipway ready for her launch, with the Black Shed at her bow, and the apprentice training centre on the left of the picture.

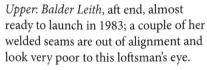

Upper: *Balder Leith*, aft end, almost ready to launch in 1983; a couple of her welded seams are out of alignment and look very poor to this loftsman's eye.

Left: *Balder Leith* takes to the water with a slight dip to starboard as she crosses the sill of the slipway.

Right: *Balder Leith* alongside after her launch ready for fitting out (Barry Booth Collection).

to Brazilian major Petrobras for four years, having started with them in 2010. She has worked constantly for the past 30 years or so.

When I went back into the yard after the *Balder Leith* had been launched, I have to say that I could see the difference. The older, more experienced, hands had mostly gone, and there was very much an attitude of *that's good enough, just get the job done*. Well, it was *not* good enough, and the following will back up my thoughts on the subject of how fast and far the yard had fallen.

You could almost feel the change in the place; some of the loftsmen had taken on new positions created in the planning department, while some others had left – and we even had a plater working in the loft! Nothing against platers – some of the best in the yard were platers – but the loft was still part of the shipwright branch of the union. I don't know how this had happened, but I suspect that, as ever, it had more to do with who you knew at the time.

The following is from Alex Eaglesham, who was superintendent of the build of *Balder Leith*, helping to give a more balanced view of how things deteriorated as time went by – the quality was just not there any more, new apprentices not being trained the same. It does not make very nice reading from my point of view, but the facts are there; while a great many very fine ships were built, some were just not as fine as they should have been.

BALDER LEITH
by Alex Eaglesham

In August 1982, I was asked by my company, Balder Offshore, if I would like the opportunity to stand by a new vessel building at Henry Robb Shipyard in Leith. This would mean re-migrating back from Canada, where my family had migrated the previous year.

I duly arrived back to find the ship construction well under way. The vessel was an Ulstein 704 Anchor Handling Supply Vessel, standard design, many of which type were used in North Sea operations. The main construction would be at H.R. but the bow and stern sections would be built on the Tyne, and the pipework, too, was sub-contracted to a Tyne company.

This was to lead to complications later on. In fact, when I arrived they were already having to renew some of the pipework due to the type of pumps H.R. had intended using. Most UT 704s used Allweiler pumps, and to get the correct pressure and volume could use a 3" pipe, But H.R. was using Hamworthy pumps, and to achieve the correct flow etc would have to use 4" pipe. But more of that later.

It also transpired that the Tyne yard had used the wrong set of drawings, so when the workers came to fit the towing forks the stiffeners were in the wrong place.

The main problem I had was the quality of steelwork, which was down to the yard personnel being either unused to reading drawings or unwilling to carry out the fabrication according to the drawing. I suspect that there was also an element of 'I have the drawings but you don't need to see them'.

The shell plate work was poorly executed, there being about 10 major faults (down one side) which delayed the launch somewhat. It was commented on by one of the yard personnel that the ship had the appearance of a Hungry Horse because of being able to see all the ribs.

Tank testing was a nightmare, especially round the recessed bilge wells – a constant battle to get a good seal.

The vessel was eventually launched just before Christmas. Some time later I was asked one Saturday morning if I would pop up and see the M.D. He had a bit of a problem; the rudder stocks had been made from the wrong material, a fact picked up by the young DNV surveyor. I was asked whether they could change them out after the trials, or should they be changed before. I reckoned if the material was too soft then best to change out before, as the ship would have to perform a very rugged hard to port/ hard to starboard manoeuvre.

Fortunately Fife Forge had two billets of the correct material, but would need the bearing sleeves from the old stocks to complete the fabrication. So the boat went back into dock, to have the rudders removed.

It was then noticed that each of the variable pitch propeller blades had large nicks in them, Ulstein from Dunfermline came across to have a look and try and find out what had happened.

The Kort nozzles that the props ran in were bought in ready for attaching to the hull (one either side); they were attached at the top onto the hull, and at the bottom supported by brackets, and between the two was what could be described as an aerofoil horizontal support.

Unfortunately when the nozzles were supplied they came with plates which penetrated the hollow section where the support was supposed to attach. The excess was then removed. The yard had decided to use all of this plate, and the support was now inside the turning circle of the props – hence the nicks, where the prop was catching on the support. Had the ship gone out on trials – remember that the engines would not be used until the boat had cleared the lock – it would have lost all four blades or at least badly damaged them. A very close shave.

It was not all gloom and doom; the pipe fitters made a very good job of running a pipe from the hydraulic header tank on the monkey island down toward the windlass, but as there was scaffolding round the bridge they worked the pipe round it. It did look a bit odd when they removed the scaffold, mind you.

The cement system required, and the drawings stated quite clearly, that there should be swept bends radius of 30 cm and a minimum distance between each bend. But the pipe guys had fitted standard bends and had put three in, one after the other. The first time cement was pumped would have resulted in a blockage, but there you go.

Carelessness also cost the ship; when they were fitting the windows in the control room the switchboard was not covered up, so a lot of the gauges suffered from grinding spatter.

Not everything was H.R.'s fault, though. One of the Caterpillar engines had a cracked liner (or leaky liner seal), and the engine had to be changed out. Unfortunately it was on the opposite side of the E.R. from the hatch.

The trials went okay, although the main engine had to be re-chocked due to a slight misalignment which showed up when the crankshaft deflections were taken with the hot engine – but as it was set in Chock Fast this was not too big a problem.

The joiners did a reasonable job of the accommodation. Although contemporary vessels use pre-built toilet/shower rooms with only the water, waste and soap to be added, H.R. had everything built on the ship. But they did a reasonable job. The only problem we had with the joinery was the bridge consoles. Normally they are sheet metal with the gauges and controls set in, but because (as they claimed)

Some of the men seen here in happier times at the yard in this photograph sent to me by Wattie. Ted Tonner, the foreman rigger, is far right.

people kept coming up with more gauges to be fitted, they were built with wood panelling. Unfortunately with the first dose of North Sea weather they collapsed.

My worst time was when I went to Montrose to see a sister vessel which had been built in Husum, in Germany, to the same spec, and I'm afraid to say that her standard of build was streets ahead.

The misalignment of such units would never have happened a few years earlier.

FOURTEEN
TWO SAINTS, THEN CLOSURE

THE END OF MORE THAN 660 YEARS OF RECORDED SHIPBUILDING AT LEITH

It is perhaps a bit outwith the remit of this book to go fully into the reasons, perceived or otherwise, as to why the shipbuilders of Leith were targeted for closure. Suffice to say that gross mis-management had a large part to play, along with an intransigent attitude in many of the workers. Add a government intent on taking the country down an entirely different future route, decimating the manufacturing industry in the process, and you will see that there can only be one outcome.

It was surely with some bitter irony and a strange twist of fate that the next order for Robbs was also the death knell for Caledon, the fine sister shipyard in Dundee that Robbs had taken over in the late 1960s. While the men of the Leith yard were working on a MacBridge unit for – of all places! – Dundee, British Shipbuilders had already decided that there would be no future for the Caledon yard, and it was closed down, with the loss of around 1,000 jobs.

The MacBridge was in fact no ship, but a unit for vehicles to be loaded from the quayside onto a ship; it was constructed on piers, and the outer end of the unit would float up and down with the tides. But this order was for some reason given a yard ship number, so it shows in the record of ships built as Ship No 528.

Welcome work, all the same, at a desperate time for the shipyard. With no orders in the books, the future did not look promising for the yard.

At a strangely busy time for the Leith Shipyards an order had come in for the build of two large ferries for the British Rail Sealink Company, another government-controlled shipping line – a fair amount of work which, it was hoped, would be the start of further orders being won by the yard, still under the umbrella of the dreaded British Shipbuilders. I'm happy to say that the problems encountered with the *Balder Leith* were not replicated on those two ships, as they were built completely at the Leith yard by Henry Robb Ltd.

While *Seaforth Sovereign* and *Balder Leith* were being built, the loft was busy running the lines for these two new ferries, yard numbers 534 and 535.

So although things were still pretty shaky in the shipyard regarding further ship orders being allocated to the yard by British Shipbuilders, the short-term order book looked good.

The ferries, to be named *St Catherine* and *St Helen*, were ro-ro passenger ferries (double-ended) for use on the routes connecting the Isle of Wight to Southampton and Portsmouth across the Solent, one of the busiest shipping routes in the world.

They had a Voith Schneider asymmetric three-propeller layout, with rudders and a skeg at both bow and stern, to avoid turning around for the return journey.

This of course was nothing new for the shipyard, as back in the 1930s it had built *South Steyne*, one of the most famous of all double-ended ferries – which is still around, berthed at Darling Harbour, Sydney, Australia.

The full-size lines for the ships were run out in what remained of the old mould loft in Leith (the tenth-scale loft having moved due to the deteriorating condition of the old building) and in preparation for the new CAD system (again, too little too late …).

I did not know at the time that I would be doing the last ever full-size lines to be done in Leith.

The build progressed against a backdrop of increasing industrial strife due to the new management trying to introduce some small changes (yet again, too little too late) and the unions continuing to hold onto outdated modes of working practices – all in a worldwide context of fewer and fewer orders being placed for ships in British yards.

Then during one particularly nasty bit of industrial strife all the shop stewards resigned. Some of the old conveners even took foremen's jobs, so while the build was going on the yard was in a bit of a mess, under the constant threat of closure.

By this time the British yards could not compete with the modern facilities and working practices of the yards in Japan and Germany. One attempt to try and close the gap was to send the loftsmen at Leith down to the headquarters of British Shipbuilders to get trained up on the new computer system, which was to eventually change the shape – literally – of shipbuilding and engineering design for ever. But again it turned out to be too little too late; once the lofting for the ferries was completed there were no further orders for the Leith yard, in spite of orders for new ships in the pipeline. So, no future ships were to be lofted on computer at Leith.

Despite all, the ferry *St Catherine* launched into the waters of the Basin of Leith Docks, where she was to be fitted out.

Known as a Saint class ship, she just looked right, and she was to serve on the route from the Isle of Wight to the

St Catherine, the first of the last two ferries.

Left: *St Catherine* tied up alongside just after her launching in 1983 (Barry Booth Collection).

Middle: The double-ended ferry *St Catherine* at the dockside in the Leith Shipyards of Henry Robb being fitted out (Barry Booth Collection).

Lower: *St Catherine* ready for fitting out: note the nice clean and clear quayside leading up to where she was berthed.

Above: *GB Conte* leaves the Solent for Italy.

Upper left: *St Catherine* repainted as *GB Conte*. (This photograph and the next one provided by Anni Reucroft, who served on the Saint class ferries built at Leith.)

Left: *GB Conte* leaves on another voyage in the evening.

mainland for almost 30 years, first with Sealink and then with Wightlink British Ferries. She was a well-known and much-loved ship, crossing the Solent in all weathers. She and her sister ship *St Helen* were at the time the largest ferries serving on this link between the Island (famous for the Cowes yachting week, and of course the Supermarine Spitfire) and the mainland.

In 2010 *St Catherine* was sold to Delcomar, a ferry company based in Italy. She was renamed *GB Conte*, and can now be seen plying her trade in what are normally warmer waters around the coast of Sardinia – and, who knows, with proper maintenance she may well last for another 20 years. She sails regularly from Palau, in the north of the island of Sardinia, to the island of La Maddalena.

The old ferry looks as good as she did when first in service almost 30 years ago, a further testament to the shipbuilders of Leith and her new owners, Delcomar.

Her current port of registry is Cagliari, and she is a huge improvement on the ships that were previously being used in the region.

This second vessel of the Saint class, *St Helen*, Ship No 535, was about 900 tonnes heavier than *St Catherine*. Amid all the industrial unrest and job uncertainty for the shipbuilders at Robbs her build went on – and there was even the carrot of the possibility of further orders being won by the yard – but *St Helen* had to be delivered on time, as we were told that Sealink had already taken summer bookings for the ship for the following season, 1984.

Other work was still going on; there was an experimental mini-submarine for the MoD (Navy) being looked at, and given the yard number of 533. Some of her lines had to be re-drawn in the loft. But the small amount of work to be carried out on that submarine would not last very long.

103

Above: The launch of *St Helen*, Ship No 535, the final ship launched from the Leith Shipyards of Henry Robb Shipbuilders and Engineers Ltd (Barry Booth Collection).

Left: *St Helen* enters the water; note the list to port!

As I completed the last drawing, the nested parts of the developed skeg, the industrial unrest was getting worse in the yard, with the men's morale at a new low point. Many were already making plans should the worst come to the worst, setting up jobs for when the axe fell.

But *St Helen* was built, and again she was a ship that just looked right although there was a small hiccup as she was launched, the port after poppets giving way as she was entering the water, giving her a bit more of a list to port than expected. But on this last launch from the Leith yard we never gave it much thought, as we just thought that ships rolled a wee bit as they went into the water.

It could have had much more serious consequences, but when she was checked out in the dry dock all was fine.

Now there was only the outfitting to be done while she was berthed alongside in the basin – and for the Black Squad of shipbuilders, this meant little or no work at all. *St Helen* was completed and handed over on time, at the end of November 1983.

The following is from one of her crew in testament to her seakeeping:

The best thing of all about the Saint class is the fact that they never, ever stop in bad weather.

It can be blowing a major storm, and while the super-modern *St Clare* has to be withdrawn in high winds, the good old Saint class will keep on running without fail.

The following is from Anni Ruecroft (senior steward) who has worked on both of the Saint class ships:

I have lived on the Isle of Wight all my life.

As a result, I have grown up with the *St Helen* and *St Catherine* always being there. Sealink, who owned them, became Wightlink in the 1990s privatisation, and I joined Wightlink as a steward in 2001. In fact, *St Helen* was actually the first ship I worked on. I am still with Wightlink, and a great many of us will be sad to see the *Helen* go.

Left: *St Helen* at Portsmouth laid up awaiting new owners (photo, Anni Ruecroft).
Right: *St Helen* sitting on the shingle and mud at the quayside at Hythe at
low tide, showing her skeg and Voith units (photo, Doug Coulson).

Upper: *Anna Mur*, ex-*St Helen*.

Above: *Anna Mur*, ex-*St Helen*, now working in the sunshine with her sister ship the ex-*St Catherine*.

The *St Helen* has now been taken over by Delcomar, and will soon be plying her trade in the warmer waters around the island of Sardinia, the same as her sister ship *St Catherine* (*GB Conte*). *St Helen* is now named the *Anna Mur*, and as I myself lofted and developed out her skegs (along with her full-size lines), they should be fine while she is at rest awaiting her new look from Delcomar, to continue her work in Sardinia.

On 19 March 2016 Delcomar held an official inauguration ceremony for the *Anna Mur* (*St Helen*) in the southern Sardinian port of Carloforte.

Joe:

I was a painter on this ship when I worked for Henry Robb in 1983 … Robbs built great ships in my time at the Leith yard … the dock is now a shopping mall called Ocean Terminal … great memories.

The dilapidated building that was the tinsmith's shop, the mould loft taking up the vast majority of the building and going back all the way. The white-painted building was the plumber's shop, with the engineering shop far right in this picture. This was just before the building, with all its maritime tradition and history, was demolished, reduced to rubble and memories (photo by Mark Young, who served his time as a tinsmith).

The winter of 1983/84 was a bad time for shipbuilders in the British Isles, and sure enough word came through in February 1984 that the famous old yard of Henry Robb Shipbuilders and Engineers was to be one of the smaller shipyards to be sacrificed, because this would help keep the larger shipyards around the country going and avert a proposed strike. The workers in the surviving larger yards also got a wage rise (all B/S of course), as most of the other yards were also closed down over a short period of time.

The empty fabrication and panel line shops in 1984, just as the yard was being closed down by order of British Shipbuilders.

Without going into all the acrimonious details of the closure this was a bad time for the whole area in general.

But nothing ever stays the same, and over time the area has been somewhat re-generated for better or worse. Some would call this social engineering on a rather grand scale, with a long-term political view to rename the town of Leith as North Edinburgh. No matter; the harsh fact remained that with the closure of the shipyard thus ended some 660 years of recorded shipbuilding history in Leith.

Not too many areas of any country could compare with this type of shipbuilding history.

Where once were shipbuilders is now a shopping centre and tourist attraction, a place where if you look really hard you may be able to find the very small plaque which says that this used to be the centre of a proud industry in this part of town, thanks to the Forth Ports Authority (photo source unknown).

The general malaise in the yard at the time and indeed in British Shipbuilders in every passing month seemed to have a negative story, and the Tory-led press, with Thatcher as the band leader, were crucifying the shipyards.

The fact that shipbuilding is always a compromise between what many believe should be and what many know is actually possible was completely wasted on politicians.

The problem was total lack of investment over many, many years, and then when the small investments were made, it was too little too late.

The yard was in fact well down the road to securing some further orders when the decision was made to close the place and to hell with the workers.

So in 1984 the yard ran out of orders and, not supported by British Shipbuilders, was given no orders to work on. The end of shipbuilding in Leith came on 27 April 1984.

All part of the Thatcherism thinking of the time. The yard was forced to close down, with the loss of around 700 direct jobs. The closure was directed by British Shipbuilders' boss Graham Day, who would go on to close down much of the car industry in the United Kingdom. He was by all accounts another person employed by government who really knew all about shipbuilding.

Further comment came to me via M.R. Ross:

The chairman of BS referred to was J Graham Day, a solicitor. He succeeded Sir Robert Atkinson. Day was appointed by Mrs T and in a meeting I attended shortly after his appointment, made it very clear that his remit was to sell the warship building yards.

I started in Robbs in Leith, but only stayed for a year before moving to Brooke Marine and finally Govan. What is missing from this paper is the international nature of shipbuilding. Keynes commented about the 'loss' we suffered from the failures of the Luftwaffe to flatten more of UK industry. The problem that bedevilled UK shipbuilding was a failure to rationalise and invest after the war in a few large yards (Robbs would have been a casualty), built around dry docks, with an internationally competitive supply chain, eg steel plate.

It was not poor industrial relations but woeful management and political neglect that sunk UK shipbuilding. Ironically we still managed to design yards in Korea and the Middle East.

The ten years until 1984 returned a total of only 19 ships, two of which were barges, along with the MacBridge unit for Dundee Port Authority, and a small experimental Navy submarine: an average of only 1.5 ships per year.

A lot of the younger men from the yard would go onto make their way in life in one way or another in industries as diverse as driving taxis to delivering the post. Some would go to jail, and some would move away or emigrate.

Some would manage to stay in the shipbuilding or ship repair industries, and some were left to just die off once the meagre redundancy money was gone. Such is life that some were pretty successful while others were not, but sure as hell if you spoke to survivors today, they would mostly agree that the Leith Shipbuilding days were good days, unlikely to be repeated in any other working environment.

Even when times ended up not very good I have had contact with ex-workers who mostly have the same good things to say about Robbs: a hell of a place to work in, but some great people. Dougie Radcliffe sent me the following:

I was not a shipwright but I worked in the loft in my first year in Robbs in 1958–59. Memories of sweeping that huge floor with damp sawdust and my first experience of machines when we took the boards down to go through the planer to take off the old scrieve lines, and Bobby Bell moaning if there were any bits of screws left in them. I realised later why he got so worked up about it. I went on to serve my time as a woodmachinist in the joiner's shop, but I was taken under Bobby Bell's wing in the carpenter's shop on quite a number of occasions. He wasn't one for working late, and I did a few all-nighters in his place when there was a docking. He did work Sunday overtime, though, and my job was to open the side door to let him out for his trip to the Peacock, and watch out for him coming back. His turned mahogany fruit bowls were legendary.

I finished my time in July 1964 and worked on for around a year before leaving the yard. I came back one more time, but I'm not sure when it was. The tug *Typhoon* was on the stocks when I started, and was launched when I was working in the loft. I remember having to go into the double bottom when she was in the fitting-out basin; they were installing some kind of gear and having to dab the chalk marks, not pleasant. Then hanging on a cradle on the side of a ship in the Imperial Dry Dock to mark up a new Plimsoll line, no health and safety. I also worked on the RFA *Engadine* when I was an apprentice, cutting all the shipsides and bulkheads, which were asbestos. I took the job, as they paid – I think it was – 6p an hour extra for working on it, and everyone thought the company was doing me a favour by giving me the extra money. But I'm suffering for it now, diagnosed with pleural plaque and folded lung.

Unfortunately many men like Dougie would end up with some serious industrial injuries, and court cases are going on to this day.

Regarding the rights and wrongs relating to the demise of a once great industry I shall leave you with the speech given in the House of Commons two days after the announced closure of the Henry Robb Shipyard at Leith.

Mr Donald Dixon, Jarrow 9:11 pm 1 February 1984

The only reason why I am winding up for the Opposition is that, unfortunately, my Hon. Friend the Member for Falkirk East (Mr Ewing) is ill. I shall try to emulate the speech that he would have made.

I was more than pleased by the speech of my Right Hon. Friend the Member for Bethnal Green and Stepney (Mr Shore). When he was first appointed Secretary of State for Trade and was in charge of shipbuilding, I had my reservations. However, Mark Twain said that when he was 16 he thought his father was a fool. By the time he was 21 he was amazed how much his father had learnt in those few short years.

I was disappointed, if not surprised, at the speech of the Secretary of State for Trade and Industry. The more I listened to him, the more I was convinced that the person was right who said that if the Prime Minister sacked him she would qualify for a Queen's Award to Industry.

Since 1979 we have had several debates on the shipbuilding industry. Unfortunately, each one has been when redundancies have been about to occur. It is the same today. I have been accused of being emotional while speaking about the shipbuilding industry. I make no apologies for that, having worked in the industry all my working life. I have lived since I was born, and still live, among the families of shipyard workers. I know the hardships which they have had to face over the years. I know the hardships which my grandparents and my father faced. It annoys me at times when I hear Conservative Members pontificating about what the workmen should do, when some of them have never seen a pair of overalls, let alone worn a pair. We have heard such speeches in the debate.

There was never a positive policy for shipbuilding until the industry was nationalised in 1977. It was taken out of the hands of private enterprise, which had lost the initiative in world markets. The industry is a classic example of the failure of competitive capitalism to create proper conditions for the workers, or the industry to benefit the economy. To hear some of the speeches made in the debate, one would think that British shipbuilding had been nationalised since the beginning of the century. It was in private hands until it was nationalised in 1977. As my Right Hon. Friend the Member for Bethnal Green and Stepney said, if it had not been nationalised in 1977, and if the Labour Government had not contracted the Polish order, there would have been no shipbuilding industry.

People talk about restrictive practices, but what they are talking about is trained men doing jobs which they are capable of doing. When we talk about demarcation, we are talking about demarcation created by the employers, not by the trade unions or the tradesmen. If the management cannot organise the electricians, plumbers and boilermakers, it is about time that the management was changed. It is not a matter of demarcation.

The Government amendment refers to privatisation. During all the years that I worked in the industry it was in private hands. The shipbuilding and ship repair industries were a jungle until nationalisation in 1977. It would turn the clock back to put the industries into private hands.

We should treat like with like when we talk about productivity. When the shipyards were in private hands, they were starved of investment, year after year. The Patton report of 1962, the Geddes report of 1966 and the Booz-Allen report of 1972 all shared a common theme – the lack of investment in the British shipbuilding industry. After the war the industry had full order books, but the owners would not invest a halfpenny. It is not so long since the men in the yards were pushing shell plates around on wooden bogies. The central problem is investment. Let us consider the equipment of the Japanese and Korean shipyards. Japan invested £600 million last year in its seven shipyards, and South Korea has invested £400 million year after year.

Too much of the recent publicity about the problems of British Shipbuilders has focused on productivity and delivery dates. The Prime Minister has accused parts of British Shipbuilders of dismal performance. The Right Hon. Lady and her Government should remember that it is not so long since they pinned a medal on one of the directors of Swan Hunters for the efforts of the 2,000 workers on the Tyne in getting the task force ready for the Falklands dispute.

Many of my colleagues were upset – and rightly so – when the secretary of State for Scotland compared the record of Britain's work force with that of the paddyfield labour force in Ayrshire. All the publicity has missed the major problem, which is the massive slump in orders being placed throughout the world. Worldwide demands have fallen from 35 million tonnes in 1975 to 14 million tonnes, and there appears to be little prospect of recovery in the immediate future. A major crisis is building up in the British yards because of the lack of orders.

Without new orders, the last delivery date for Govan Shipyard is April 1984; for Smiths Docks, June 1984; and for Austin and Pickersgill, December 1984. The engine build capacity is also in serious trouble, as was mentioned by my Hon. Friends the Members for Sunderland North (Mr Clay) and for Sunderland South (Mr Baiger). The Government must address themselves to the workload crisis.

The trade unions have co-operated with British Shipbuilders to raise productivity. According to the chairman of British Shipbuilders, the new agreement will raise productivity to a level on a par with that of northern European yards. It is a pity that the chairman did not show the concern expressed by the trade unions when the industry was threatened with a national strike on 6 January. Mr Day went on holiday to Canada for three weeks and left the union negotiators to sort out the problems with a director. That is not the sort of behaviour that we expect from someone who is responsible for a vital industry.

A great deal of nonsense is talked about high wages. A recent survey carried out by a trade union at a British Shipbuilders' establishment showed that 62 per cent of the manual workers were in receipt of some form of state benefit. During the period when the shipyard workers fell from 3rd to 19th in the wages league, the members of the board looked after their money. The 1981 report showed that the 17 full-time and part-time members cost £215,000. In the 1982–83 report, the figure was £398,618 for the 14 part-time and full-time board members. In effect, the average payment for the board members of British Shipbuilders increased from £12,681 in 1980 to £28,472 in 1983 – an increase of 128 per cent at the same time the workers dropped from 3rd place to 19th in the wages league.

There is a view in certain parts of the House that the taxpayer would be better off if British Shipbuilders were allowed to disappear, in view of the losses that it is making. That view is factually wrong, and it displays, too, a callous disregard for the fate of the workers and their families. This year British Shipbuilders had a wages bill of about £500 million. As a consequence it paid to the Exchequer a total of £180 million in income tax and national insurance. British Shipbuilders stands to lose £120 million. That is a drain on the Exchequer, but in net terms the Exchequer is still £60 million better off than it would be if the industry were to die.

If the industry did not exist, £280 million in exports would be lost. Sixty per cent of the cost of a ship is for materials, and that is not accounted for by British Shipbuilders. Nearly all of that is supplied by United Kingdom families. If the industry did not exist, 30,000 people making steel, engines and other components would not be needed. They would no longer pay at least £100 million a year in income tax and national insurance.

Those who say that money spent on the shipbuilding industry should be spent elsewhere are wrong. If the industry disappeared, the Exchequer would lose receipts of £280 million in order to save the £120 million which it is paying in subsidies at the moment. That is economics gone crazy. The taxpayer would not be better off; he would be worse off by £160 million. One must also consider the cost of maintaining 90,000 people on the dole. It costs £6,000 a year to keep a shipyard worker out of work. It costs £6,000 to subsidise him in the present state of world shipping.

The Government, the media and the nation must stop being complacent about the disastrous situation in the industry. They must stop saying that it would be a blessing in disguise if the industry were to disappear. The situation is critical, not just for the workers, but for the future of the industrial base and for our ability to create exports and maintain social services.

We want action to stop the lifeblood draining away from the industry. By October 1983, 30,000 jobs had been lost. In October 1983 British Shipbuilders announced another 2,069 redundancies. In January 1984 the rundown of Scott Lithgow was announced, with another 4,000 job losses. Last Wednesday a further 1,872 job losses were announced, with three yard closures – Cleland's, Henry Robb and Goole.

The Hon. Member for Tynemouth (Mr Trotter) and my Hon. Friend the Member for Edinburgh, Leith (Mr Brown) referred to Henry Robb. *The Observer* of 10 October 1983 said:

'As attempts are made to avert a national strike in British Shipbuilders, three yards face closure – because of an unexplained hold-up in accepting £50 million worth of naval orders. Contracts for at least 14 ships are in the pipeline from the Ministry of Defence – and they seem tailor-made for the three small yards, Henry Robb at Leith, Cleland's at Wallsend and Goole on Humberside. But BS has said that 1,500 workers face redundancy because of a lack of fresh orders at the yards which will run out of existing work within a few weeks. Despite renewed assurances from BS that work for the yards is being actively sought, it appears acceptance of the orders is being deliberately delayed to get the closures out of the way.'

I am convinced that British Shipbuilders decided to close Cleland's last October. British Shipbuilders deliberately delayed placing the orders there. There was an ash carrier for the CEGB. British Shipbuilders had the letter of intent in November. The technical drawings were done, yet the order was transferred to another yard. I believe that if there were a national strike, Mr Day would say that Cleland's would not open its gates again.

The Government's response has been inadequate. There is overcapacity in every country. Each country is taking measures to buy work. Prices offered by the Asian yards are 35 per cent lower than those offered by British shipbuilders. In the *Financial Times* on 25 January there was an article about the problems faced by the French. It was reported that the French Government had decided to give the French shipbuilding industry an additional £290 million to £330 million in subsidy this year, and had blocked an order from a French shipping company for four ships from a Yugoslav shipyard.

My Hon. Friend the Member for Sunderland South said that Japanese shipowners had placed orders for 113 cargo ships to keep the Japanese shipbuilding industry going. All kinds of attractive credit arrangements are being offered. Other countries are buying their way out of their problems. The Government are incapable of appreciating the point, or they do not care.

How long will British Shipbuilders fight according to the Marquess of Queensberry rules when every other country is involved in all-in wrestling? The Government are like the little boy standing on the burning deck. They are pursuing a policy of privatising warship yards where there is Ministry of Defence work, but they have no policy for the others.

A concerted policy of intervention is needed to protect the nation's vital interests. As my Right Hon. Friend the Member for Bethnal Green and Stepney said, we are an island nation dependent upon our maritime industry for our survival and defence. We live on an island in a world which is two thirds covered by water. About 90 per cent of the value of our trade is carried by ships. It is essential for us to have a shipping industry and the capability to build and maintain the ships.

British shipowners such as Cunard and P & O and operators in the North Sea must be persuaded to place orders in British yards. The Government have a range of carrots and sticks which they could use. Tax relief on ships built in non-EEC yards must be removed. Incentives must be offered to place work in British yards. Shipbuilding communities, the Exchequer and the taxpayer would benefit.

There will be jobs on the Sun Oil contract for Cammell Laird and the BP advanced SWOP project, and the renewal of the QE2's engines is being discussed. Those jobs must be placed in British yards to keep them busy. Only then can the work force produce the high levels of efficiency which have been asked for by British Shipbuilders.

The Government-owned British Shipbuilders Britoil said that three quarters of the blame for the problems with its contract at Scott Lithgow was down to bad management. We have heard enough about blaming the work force for that. It is a problem which British Shipbuilders' owners must cure. The Government must stop making statements which undermine customer confidence in British Shipbuilders. The industry can and will deliver. It needs Government support and coherent policies to enable it to survive. Without that it cannot survive, whatever efforts are made by the dwindling work force.

My Right Hon. Friend the Member for Bethnal Green and Stepney spoke about the social consequences of closures. There is a close relationship in shipbuilding communities between the working and living environment. There is a remarkably strong community spirit among shipbuilding workers. For example, a survey conducted not so many years ago showed that at the Swan Hunter Wallsend yard, 62 per cent of the work force either lived in Wallsend or adjacent towns. The situation on Wearside is even more marked. A survey of the work force in Austin and Pickersgill showed that 37 per cent lived within one mile of the yard and that only 5 per cent lived more than five miles away.

Some people say that Graham Day and his board are Shipbuilding Security reincarnated. Let me enlighten those Hon. Members who do not know about Shipbuilding Security. That organisation was set up in the 1930s and comprised merchant bankers, shipowners and shipbuilders. At that time there was overcapacity and a world slump, and they went around the country, bought the shipyards, closed them down and sold the assets, with no worry about the social consequences.

Those vultures came to Jarrow in 1934 and bought the Jarrow shipyard. It was subsequently closed and a 40-year embargo was placed on the building of ships. Afterwards, Ellen Wilkinson wrote a book called *The Town that was Murdered: The Life Story of Jarrow*. My father and grandfather were two of the 5,000 men who were thrown on the scrap heap in 1934. My grandfather never worked again. My father did, in 1939 when the ships were needed, and if he refused to work overtime he appeared before a tribunal and was fined. The ships were not needed in 1934 but they were needed in 1939. The same can be said of the Falklands campaign, when the workers were praised by the Prime Minister and some of her Cabinet colleagues.

For a long time Tyne and Wear county council has conducted a 'Save Our Shipyards' campaign. Had the Secretary of State for Industry and the Minister of State done as much as Michael Campbell and Jim Cousins – the leader and deputy leader of Tyne and Wear County Council – the industry would not be in its present state. Tyne and Wear has tried in every way to attract orders for the shipbuilding industry. It is a pity that the Government do not take a leaf out of its book.

Not so long ago P & O placed a £90 million order for one of the largest cruise liners ever to be built, and that went to Finland. When my Right Hon. Friend the

Member for Manchester Gorton (Mr Kaufman) wrote to the Prime Minister, she replied that that order could not be placed with British Shipbuilders because we did not have the finishing trades to carry it out. What nonsense. Joiners, electricians, plumbers and so on are out of work in the Tyne and Wear area.

We require a relaxation of the financial limits and the maintenance of the intervention board at an adequate level. There must be incentives for British shipowners to have their ships built in British yards. We must maximise United Kingdom offshore orders for the North Sea oil and gas industries. There must be long-term planning for public sector ordering, especially for naval vessels. We must introduce a scrap and build policy to upgrade British shipbuilding standards and to accelerate orders for new ships.

Those are the things that the Government should do. They should not repeatedly blame the workers for the problems now faced by the shipbuilding industry. The Opposition are concerned about the industry. That is why my Right Hon. Friend the Leader of the Opposition will visit the Tyne on 27 February at the invitation of the GMBATU. He will speak to the shipbuilding workers, because he is more concerned than the Government about the plight of the industry and the shipbuilding communities.

As an island race we depend on exports and imports for our survival. Therefore, it is indisputable that the main form of transport is by sea, and that means ships. Our ability to build those ships is of the utmost importance to our economic and strategic survival.

Nobody doubts, on the defence side, that we should build vessels for our Navy. Everybody with knowledge of the industry agrees that merchant shipping, naval building, ship repairing and engine building are all part of the whole, and that the condition of one affects the others. It would be absolute nonsense to sell off the warship yards and expect merchant shipbuilding to survive, and I hope that the Minister will say something positive in reply to the debate.

Questions need to be answered about Tyne Shiprepairers. It was said that that yard had gone through a traumatic experience when it was nationalised. In fact, British ship repairers were not nationalised in 1977. The shipbuilding industry was nationalised, and the ship repairing industry volunteered to be nationalised. The shop stewards at Tyne Shiprepairers have estimated that the entitlement under the shipbuilding redundancy scheme for the employees there totals £10·7 million. There has been a £4·2 million buy-out. What has happened to the £6·5 million of redundancy money to which the 985 workers are entitled?

May we be told how much the owners of Tyne Shiprepairers paid for that industry? Were the two directors who bought it out on British Shipbuilders' payroll? Are Abbott and Burns the only directors of Tyne Shiprepairers, or are there other directors who are still employed by British Shipbuilders with an interest in Tyne Shiprepairers? I hope that the Minister will answer those and other questions, and comment on the constructive suggestions that my Right Hon. Friends have made in the debate.

Sadly, anyone involved in the British shipbuilding industry at the time knew the government's answer to the above questions!

How a once great industry was cast aside by outsiders! I could not have put it any better myself. And all this for what, I have to ask myself, as I look around this industry that I am still fortunate enough to be involved in. No more, though, will men be trained in the art of shipbuilding at Leith – we had been well and truly sold down the river.

Another point of interest is the fact that for several decades the quango British Shipbuilders Ltd was kept going, paying out good money to the good folks in the House of Lords who were still on the board of that total waste-of-time company. It continued to operate for many years, principally in order to deal with all the claims and pensions coming in from former shipbuilders who in the course of their work had contracted deadly diseases such as asbestosis, deafness, white finger, lead poisoning and the like.

Of course, due to stalling tactics not much has been paid out to the very few workers that still survive, but what the quango did pay out was salaries and such to those who administered it for 30 or so years. Thankfully it was wound up in 2017. I am not sure what happened to any money still in its coffers at the time.

As I come to the end of this book it is difficult for me to be objective over the decisions made more than 40 years ago. Some may say we're all wise with hindsight – but the results of the moves made at that time to decimate the shipbuilding industry have cost us since then, and are still costing us, as ours is an island nation, built on ships and the sea. The final irony must be that we are now hearing from the self-same government as they attempt to try and correct what they call in England the north–south divide. They are spending billions of taxpayers' money to re-industrialise the north. At times I wonder if we ever learn from history!

I leave it to you to form your own conclusions.

The Loftsman

LIST OF SHIPS BUILT BY HENRY ROBB SHIPBUILDERS & ENGINEERS LTD

The following pages show the complete list of ships built from the opening of the Henry Robb Shipyard in April 1918 to the forced closure of the shipyard in April 1984. The list is compiled just as the shipyard order book shows, minus the ships built during the Second World War, which will form the subject of another book that I will add to this series.

The list is compiled in the order of each vessel's allocated number, not the date she was launched, so you will see some vessels high on the list that were not in fact launched until much later, due to factors such as priority given to which ships were needed the quickest.

Ship No	Name	Dimensions	Tonnage	Type	Launched
1	-	50 × 11 × 4.3 ft	23	Pontoon	1918
2	-	55 × 19 × 5	42	SP Pontoon	1918
3	-	60 × 27 × 7	113	Pontoon	1918
4	-	50 × 11 × 4.3	23	Pontoon	1918
5	-	50 × 11 × 4.3	23	Pontoon	1918
6	-	66 × 16.6 × 6.9	60	Dumb Barge	1919
7	-	66 × 16.6 × 6.9	60	Dumb Barge	1919
8	-	120 × 25 × 9	227	Dumb Barge	1919
9	-	32 × 9.6 × 3.6	10	Pontoon	1919
10	-	32 × 9.6 × 3.6	10	Pontoon	1919
11	-	50 × 10.4 × 4.6	23	Pontoon	1920
12	-	50 × 10.4 × 4.6	67	Pontoon	1920
13	-	62.6 × 12.6 × 5.9	38	Dumb Barge	1920
14	-	69.11 × 6.95 × 3.11	17	Pontoon	1921
15	-	80 × 17 × 7.6	84	Dumb Barge	1921
16	WESTMERE	60 × 16 × 7.6	44	Tug	1921

Ship No	Name	Dimensions	Tonnage	Type	Launched
17	*BHAVSINHJI*	139.6 × 29.6 × 12.9	443	T.S. Grab Dredger	1922
18		65 × 23.6 × 6.6	81	Pontoon	1923
19		65 × 25 × 5.6	65	SP Pontoon	1924
20	*FAIRPORT*	78.6 × 19.6 × 7.3	91	Dredger	1925
21	*W. MESSINA*	90 × 20 × 11	121	Tug	12/03/1925
22	-	85 × 20 × 7.6	85	Dumb Barge	1925
23	-	85 × 20 × 7.6	85	Dumb Barge	1925
24	-	85 × 20 × 7.6	85	Dumb Barge	1925
25	-	85 × 20 × 7.6	85	Dumb Barge	1925
26	-	85 × 20 × 7.6	85	Dumb Barge	1925
27	-	85 × 20 × 7.6	85	Dumb Barge	1925
28	-	85 × 20 × 7.6	85	Dumb Barge	1925
29	-	85 × 20 × 7.6	85	Dumb Barge	1925
30	*L.S. ALBATROSS*	102 × 24.3 × 13.4	253	Light Ship	20/10/1925
31	-	62.6 × 12.6 × 5.9	38	Dumb Barge	1925
32	-	75 × 25 × 8	120	Dumb Barge	1925
33	-	75 × 25 × 8	120	Dumb Barge	1925
34	-	62.6 × 12.6 × 5.9	38	Dumb Barge	1925
35	*RUKAMAVATI*	139.6 × 29.6 × 12.9	412	S.S. Grab Dredger	15/12/1925
36	-	70 × 16 × 2.6	28	River Ferry	1926
37	-	85 × 20 × 7.6	85	Dumb Barge	1926
38	-	85 × 20 × 7.6	85	Dumb Barge	1926
39	-	85 × 20 × 7.6	85	Dumb Barge	1926
40	-	85 × 20 × 7.6	85	Dumb Barge	1926
41	-	125 × 30 × 8	250	Coaling Lighter	1926
42	-	125 × 30 × 8	250	Coaling Lighter	1926
43	-	85 × 24 × 7	114	Dumb Barge	1926
44	-	85 × 24 × 7	114	Crane Barge	1926
45	-	85 × 20 × 7.6	85	Dumb Barge	1926
46	-	85 × 20 × 7.6	85	Dumb Barge	1926
47	-	85 × 20 × 7.6	85	Dumb Barge	1926
48	-	85 × 20 × 7.6	85	Dumb Barge	1926
49	-	85 × 20 × 7.6	85	Dumb Barge	1926
50	-	85 × 20 × 7.6	85	Dumb Barge	1926

Ship No	Name	Dimensions	Tonnage	Type	Launched
51	-	63 × 15.6 × 7.6	58	Dumb Barge	1926
52	-	63 × 15.6 × 7.6	58	Dumb Barge	1926
53	-	63 × 15.6 × 7.6	58	Dumb Barge	1926
54	-	63 × 15.6 × 7.6	58	Dumb Barge	1927
55	-	63 × 15.6 × 7.6	58	Dumb Barge	1927
56	-	63 × 15.6 × 7.6	58	Dumb Barge	1927
57	-	63 × 15.6 × 7.6	58	Oil Barge	1927
58	-	95 × 24 × 7.6	140	Dumb Barge	1927
59	-	95 × 24 × 7.6	140	Crane Barge	1927
60	G	170 × 36 × 12.6	591	S.P. Hopper Barge	03/05/1927
61	H	170 × 36 × 12.6	591	S.P. Hopper Barge	15/06/1927
62	LAKSHMI	120 × 20 × 6	80	T.S. Passenger Vessel	1927
63	CLEAR WELL	95 × 23 × 8	139	Hopper Barge	03/02/1927
64	-	110 × 28 × 8.6	210	Dumb Barge	
65	-	110 × 28 × 8.6	210	Dumb Barge	1927
66	-	85 × 24 × 7	114	Dumb Barge	1927
67	-	85 × 24 × 7	114	Dumb Barge	1927
68	-	36 × 12 × 5.6	18	Mooring Lighter	1927
69	SIR DESMOND O'CALLAGHAN	75 × 18 × 7	66	S.S. Tender	31/05/1927
70	-	72 × 20 × 6.6	71	Dumb Barge	1927
71	-	72 × 20 × 6.6	71	Dumb Barge	1927
72	-	72 × 20 × 6.6	71	Dumb Barge	1927
73	-	72 × 20 × 6.6	71	Dumb Barge	1927
74	-	60 × 18.6 × 7.6	63	Sand Hopper Dredger	1927
75	LENA W	65.6 × 16 × 8	57	S.S. Tug	26/08/1927
76	BUSI	75 × 18 × 9	80	S.S. Tug	30/09/1927
77	-	70 24.6 × 7	58	Crane Pontoon	
78	ULUNDI	75 × 18 × 10.6	97	S.S. Tug/Pilot	16/09/1927
79	BRANKSEA	62 × 23 × 7	68	Grab Dredger	17/09/1927
80	JERSEY	40 × 11.9 × 5.11	14	Motor Tug	02/09/1927
81	SATURNO	108 × 24 × 12	213	Twin Screw Tug	22/05/1928

Ship No	Name	Dimensions	Tonnage	Type	Launched
82	-	73 × 18 × 7.6	75	Dumb Barge	1928
83	-	73 × 18 × 7.6	75	Dumb Barge	1928
84	-	73 × 18 × 7.6	75	Dumb Barge	1928
85	-	73 × 18 × 7.6	75	Dumb Barge	1928
86	-	73 × 18 × 7.6	75	Dumb Barge	1928
87	-	73 × 18 × 7.6	75	Dumb Barge	1928
88	-	60 × 18 × 6.6	57	Dumb Barge	1928
89	-	60 × 18 × 6.6	57	Dumb Barge	1928
90	-	55 × 10.6 × 5.3	21	Dumb Barge	1928
91	-	22 × 13 × 3.6	8	Crane Pontoon	1928
92	-	55 × 16.6 × 7	50	Barge	1928
93	-	55 × 16.6 × 7	50	Barge	1928
94	-	55 × 16.6 × 7	50	Barge	1928
95	-	55 × 16.6 × 7	50	Barge	1928
96	*CARANDA*	201.8 × 36.3 × 11.6	776	Cargo Dumb Lighter	1928
97	-	73 × 18 × 7.6	75	Lighter	1928
98	-	73 × 18 × 7.6	75	Lighter	1928
99	-	73 × 18 × 7.6	75	Lighter	1928
100	-	73 × 18 × 7.6	75	Lighter	1928
101	-	73 × 18 × 7.6	75	Lighter	1928
102	-	73 × 18 × 7.6	75	Lighter	1928
103	-	68 × 35 × 4.6	85	Grab Dredger	1928
104	-	68 × 35 × 4.6	85	Concrete Mill	1928
105	-	70 × 24.6 × 7	90	Crane Pontoon	1928
106	-	70 × 24.6 × 7	90	Crane Pontoon	1928
107	-	70 × 24.6 × 7	90	Crane Pontoon	1928
108	*FOREMOST 49*	157.6 × 32 × 14	564	Bucket Dredger	12/10/1928
109	*MUDA*	76.8 × 18 × 9	83	S.S. Tug	07/08/1927
110	*IAPETUS*	95 × 24 × 7.6	140	Lighter	29/06/1928
111	*ENCELADUS*	95 × 24 × 7.6	140	Lighter	29/06/1928
112	*AGUARAY*	160 × 34 × 8.6	468	T.S. Motor Lighter	12/09/1928
113	*PORT WAIKATO*	180 × 28.9 × 13.3	668	Motor Vessel	01/10/1929
114	*W5*	95 × 24 × 7.6	140	Lighter	1929

Ship No	Name	Dimensions	Tonnage	Type	Launched
115	*W6*	95 × 24 × 7.6	140	Lighter	1929
116	-	73 × 23 × 24.6	220	Dock Caisson (Prince of Wales Dry Dock)	1929
117	-	90 × 21.6 × 7	108	Lighter	1929
118	-	63 × 15.6 × 7.6	56	Lighter	1929
119	-	63 × 15.6 × 7.6	56	Lighter	1929
120	-	63 × 15.6 × 7.6	56	Lighter	1929
121	-	63 × 15.6 × 7.6	56	Lighter	1929
122	-	63 × 15.6 × 7.6	56	Lighter	1929
123	-	63 × 15.6 × 7.6	56	Lighter	1929
124	-	40 × 15 × 6	33	Barge (Swim Ends)	1929
125	*CHUN PING*	139.6 × 29.6 × 12.9	426	Twin Grab Hopper Dredger	28/12/1928
126	-	53 × 16.4 × 5	35	Pumping Barge	1929
127	-	53 × 16.4 × 5	35	Pumping Barge	1929
128	*MONTERIA*	140 × 27 × 7.6	287	T.S.M.V. Passenger & Cargo	15/03/1929
129	-	50 × 12 × 4.6	75	Barge	1929
130	-	73 × 18 × 7.6	75	Water carrying lighter	1929
131	-	73 × 18 × 7.6	75	Water carrying lighter	1929
132	-	50 × 33.8 × 6	85	Cargo Pontoon	1929
133	-	50 × 33.8 × 6	85	Cargo Pontoon	1929
134	*PHAROS*	125 × 27 × 14	303	T.S. Salvage Tug	28/05/1929
135	-	70 × 27 × 4.6	68	Grab Dredger	1929
136	-	80 × 32 × 4.6	92	Grab Dredger	1929
137	-	50.3 × 17.2 × 6.3	45	Sugar Carrying Barge	1929
138	-	50.3 × 17.2 × 6.3	45	Sugar Carrying Barge	1929
139	-	50.3 × 17.2 × 6.3	45	Sugar Carrying Barge	1929

Ship No	Name	Dimensions	Tonnage	Type	Launched
140	*SEMBAWANG* (J.J.10)	118 × 32 × 10	316	Paddle Train Ferry	1929
141	*LUNCHU* (J.J.11)	118 × 32 × 10	316	Paddle Train Ferry	1929
142	*TOLVERNE*	115 × 25 × 7.6	164	Grab Hopper Dredger	30/08/1929
143	*LOCHSHIEL*	105 × 26 × 9.6	208	Motor Cargo Vessel	08/08/1929
144	-	87 × 17.6 × 4.1	45	Oil Lighter	1929
145	-	87 × 17.6 × 4.1	45	Oil Lighter	1929
146	-	87 × 17.6 × 4.1	45	Oil Lighter	1929
147	-	87 × 17.6 × 4.1	45	Oil Lighter	1929
148	-	87 × 17.6 × 4.1	45	Oil Lighter	1929
149	-	87 × 17.6 × 4.1	45	Oil Lighter	1929
150	-	87 × 17.6 × 4.1	45	Oil Lighter	1929
151	-	87 × 17.6 × 4.1	45	Oil Lighter	1929
152	-	65 × 21 × 7	60	Grab Hopper Dredger	1929
153	*DENESE*	40 × 11.9 × 5.11	13	S.S. Tug	13/09/1927
154	*BOMBO*	154 × 30 × 14.2	603	S.S. Motor Coaster	18/12/1929
155	*S. PAULO*	110 × 29.6 × 13.6	263	T.S. Salvage Tug	02/04/1930
156	*CATALPA*	201.8 × 36.3 × 10.6	775	Cargo Dumb Lighter	13/02/1930
157	*CEDRINA*	201.8 × 36.3 × 10.6	775	Cargo Dumb Lighter	21/03/1930
158	-	50 × 21 × 5	50	Grab Dredger Pontoon	1930
159	*JJ 13*	65 × 26 × 6	90	Grab Dredger Pontoon	1930
160	*KATHARINE II*	114 × 22 × 8	180	T.S. Motor Vessel	01/05/1930
161	-	74 × 20 × 7	80	Sugar Lighter	1930
162	-	74 × 20 × 7	80	Sugar Lighter	1930
163	-	74 × 20 × 7	80	Sugar Lighter	1930
164	-	50.3 × 17.2 × 6.3	45	Sugar Lighter	1930

Ship No	Name	Dimensions	Tonnage	Type	Launched
165	*AJUDANTE*	60 × 15 × 7	105	Single Screw Tug	28/07/1930
166	-	75 × 20 × 9.6	105	Cargo Lighter	1930
167	-	75 × 20 × 9.6	105	Cargo Lighter	1930
168	-	75 × 20 × 9.6	105	Cargo Lighter	1930
169	-	75 × 20 × 9.6	105	Cargo Lighter	1930
170	-	75 × 20 × 9.6	105	Cargo Lighter	1930
171	-	75 × 20 × 9.6	105	Cargo Lighter	1930
172	-	75 × 20 × 9.6	105	Cargo Lighter	1930
173	-	75 × 20 × 9.6	105	Cargo Lighter	1930
174	-	75 × 20 × 9.6	105	Cargo Lighter	1930
175	-	75 × 20 × 9.6	105	Cargo Lighter	1930
176	*TARRAFAL*	110 × 26.6 × 11	257	S.S. Water Carrier	26/08/1930
177	-	133 × 23 × 9	220	Hopper Barge	1930
178	-	133 × 23 × 9	220	Hopper Barge	1930
179	-	133 × 23 × 9	220	Hopper Barge	1930
180	*WEAR GRAB DREDGER No 2*	92 × 32 × 11	275	Saddle Back Grab Hopper Dredger	08/10/1930
181	*AGUILA*	260 × 42 × 13	1369	T.S. Motor Cargo Vessel	08/12/1930
182	-	53 × 16.4 × 5	35	Pumping Barge	1930
183	-	80 × 32 × 4.6	92	Grab Dredger	1930
184	*SCOT II*	75 × 15 × 8.6	59	S.S. Tug	19/03/1931
185	*KASHAN*	160 × 25 × 8.6	309	Cargo Lighter	1931
186	*KAZVIN*	160 × 25 × 8.6	309	Cargo Lighter	1931
187	*No 187*	164 × 29.6 × 7.10	335	Dumb Train Ferry	1931
188	*No 188*	164 × 29.6 × 7.10	335	Dumb Train Ferry	1931
189	*LAFONIA*	165 × 32.6 × 13.6	768	Passenger & Cargo Vessel	18/08/1931
190	*SHEILA OF PENRYN*	67 × 18 × 7.3	50	Motor Grab Dredger	28/05/1931
191	*MIRA*	65 × 16.6 × 8	66	S.S. Tug	28/07/1931
192	*GOTHLAND*	250 × 38 × 24.9	1286	Passenger & Cargo Steamer	09/03/1932

Ship No	Name	Dimensions	Tonnage	Type	Launched
193	HMS *BISHOPSGATE*	93 × 26 × 13.6	210	Gate Lifting Vessel	15/11/1932
193a	HMS *ALDGATE*	-	210	Netlayer	1933
193b	HMS *WATERGATE*	-	210	Netlayer	1933
194	*THE MILLER*	85 × 19 × 8.3	118	Motor Coaster	05/07/1932
195	*COCHIN*	110 × 29.6 × 13.6	273	T.S. Salvage Tug	14/02/1933
196	*WAVERLEY*	35 × 9.6 × 4.2	10	Motor Cabin Cruiser	1933
197	*LECTRO*	86 × 22 × 11.6	120	S.S. Diesel Electric Tug	21/09/1933
198	*BRITISH COAST*	230 × 35 × 21.6	888	T.S. Motor Cargo Vessel	04/11/1933
199	*JANARDAN*	160 × 27 × 9	299	Motor Grab Dredger	06/09/1933
200	*LUCAYAN*	65 × 21 × 7	64.4	Motor Grab Dredger	26/09/1933
201	*RIO*	75 × 20 × 9.0	80	Single Screw Diesel Tug	09/10/1934
202	-	74 × 24 × 8.6	120	Water Barge	1934
203	-	74 × 24 × 8.6	120	Water Barge	1934
204	*ATLANTIC COAST*	230 × 35 × 21.6	889	T.S. Motor Cargo Vessel	16/05/1934
205	*GOLDEN GRAIN*	82 × 17.3 × 8.3	102	Motor Coaster	17/03/1934
206	*ANNABELLA*	64.3 × 14 × 8.3	43	T.S. Motor Yacht	14/07/1934
207	*MUNMORAH*	230 × 35 × 21.6	1273	S.S. Collier	09/08/1934
208	-	156 × 26.6 × 11	200	Barge	1934
209	-	156 × 26.6 × 11	200	Barge	1934
210	*NORA*	88 × 22.6 × 11	135	S.S. Tug	28/08/1934
211	-	40 × 11.9 × 5.11	15	Motor Tug	1934
212	MSC *FIREFLY*	90 × 24 × 12	176	S.S. Tug	02/05/1935
213	-	36 × 10 × 4.6	14	Steel Barge	1935
214	HMS *BASSET*	150 × 27.6 × 14.6	433	Armed Trawler	28/09/1935
215	*OCEAN COAST*	250 × 38 × 22.9	1173	T.S. Motor Cargo Vessel	31/07/1935
216	*ARGOS*	285 × 50 × 14	1974	T.S. Motor Cargo Vessel	26/09/1935

Ship No	Name	Dimensions	Tonnage	Type	Launched
217	-	40 × 12 × 6	23	Hopper Barge	1935
218	BHIMSEN	86.6 × 22 × 10.6	141	S.S. Tug	12/10/1935
219	-	38 × 18.6 × 4.6	30	Pontoon	1935
220	ST ANTHONY	180 × 32 × 17	452	Twin Screw Passenger Vessel	25/01/1936
221	-	80 × 23 × 6.6	78	Grab Hopper Dredger	
222	GENERAL IV	65 × 16.6 × 8.6	50	Motor Tug	26/02/1936
223	-	38 × 18.6 × 4.6	28	Pontoon	1936
224	-	65 × 21 × 7	64	Grab Hopper Dredger	1936
225	GEORGE SALT	75 × 19 × 9	77	S.S. Motor Tug	07/05/1936
226	ABEILLE No 8	125 × 32 × 14	402	S.S. Tug	07/04/1936
227	PEMBROKE COAST	199 × 34 × 21	625	T.S. Motor Cargo Vessel	18/06/1936
228	ESK	95 × 25 × 7.6	125	Grab Hopper Dredger	17/09/1936
229	GALLIONS REACH	178 × 34 × 17.6	796	Steam Hopper	20/08/1936
230	-	38 × 18.6 × 4.6	31	Pontoon	1936
231	-	85 × 21 × 5.6	85	Barge	1936
232	-	85 × 21 × 5.6	85	Barge	1936
233	-	33 × 18 × 4	20	Pontoon	1936
234	MULUBINBA		1262	Cargo Steamer	
235	PORT TAURANGA	235 × 45 × 15.6	1524	TS MV	26/11/1936
236	LOCKWOOD	175 × 28.6 × 17	633	S.S. Motor Cargo Vessel	19/10/1936
237	ROOKWOOD	175 × 28.6 × 17	633	S.S. Motor Cargo Vessel	01/10/1936
238	POWER CHIEF	130 × 26 × 13.3	444	Oil Tanker	11/02/1937
239	A.I.O.C. 19	68 × 20 × 5.9	60	Oil Carrying Barge	1937
240	LOCHEE	223 × 36 × 22	964	S.S. Motor Cargo Vessel	08/07/1937
241	SOFALA	230 × 36 × 22	1031	T.S. Motor Cargo Vessel	25/08/1937
242	A.A. COWAN	125 × 24 × 9.6	295	T.S. Motor Cargo Vessel	01/12/1937

Ship No	Name	Dimensions	Tonnage	Type	Launched
243	JOSEPH FLINT	136 × 24 × 9.6	320	T.S. Motor Cargo Vessel	10/08/1937
244	SPINEL	175 × 28.6 × 17	650	S.S. Motor Cargo Vessel	08/09/1937
245	MV KAHIKA	235 × 45 × 15.6	1536	T.S. Motor Cargo Vessel	17/12/1937
246	JACINTH	175 × 28.6 × 17	650	S.S. Motor Cargo Vessel	20/11/1937
247	HMS MASTIFF	150 × 27 × 15	520	Armed Trawler	17/02/1938
248	-	125 × 27 × 6.6	125	Dumb Barge	1938
249	-	125 × 27 × 6.6	125	Dumb Barge	1938
250	-	125 × 27 × 6.6	125	Dumb Barge	1938
251	-	125 × 27 × 6.6	125	Dumb Barge	1938
252	-	125 × 27 × 6.6	125	Dumb Barge	1938
253	-	125 × 27 × 6.6	125	Dumb Barge	1938
254	-	125 × 27 × 6.6	125	Dumb Barge	1938
255	-	125 × 27 × 6.6	125	Dumb Barge	1938
256	-	125 × 27 × 6.6	125	Dumb Barge	1938
257	-	125 × 27 × 6.6	125	Dumb Barge	1938
258	-	80 × 19 × 5.3	75	Dumb Barge	1938
259	-	80 × 19 × 5.3	75	Dumb Barge	1938
260	-	80 × 19 × 5.3	75	Dumb Barge	1938
261	-	80 × 19 × 5.3	75	Dumb Barge	1938
262	CUBAHAMA	250 × 38 × 21	932	T.S. Motor Cargo Vessel	28/06/1938
263	HMS REDSTART	145 × 27 × 14	425	Indicator Loop Mine Layer	03/05/1938
264	HMS RINGDOVE	145 × 27 × 14	425	Indicator Loop Mine Layer	16/06/1938
265	MSC ARCHER	86 × 23 × 12	144	Single Screw Tug	29/04/1938
266	MSC ARROW	86 × 23 × 12	144	Single Screw Tug	26/07/1938
267	SS SOUTH STEYNE	220 × 38 × 15.9	1203	Double Ended Steam Ferry	01/04/1938
268	MV KOPARA	190 × 35.6 21.3	679	T.S. Motor Cargo Vessel	30/07/1938
269	MV KARITANE	275 × 45 × 21.6	2534	T.S. Motor Cargo Vessel	21/12/1938

Ship No	Name	Dimensions	Tonnage	Type	Launched
270	SERTANEJO	88 × 17.3 × 4	85	Stern Wheeler	1938
271	-	85 × 16 × 4.6	85	Barge	1938
272	-	85 × 16 × 4.6	85	Barge	1938
273	MV PURIRI	180 × 35 × 14	927	Motor Cargo Vessel	25/10/1938
274	KANGAN	160 × 25 × 8.6	309	Dumb Barge	25/08/1938
275	KARIND	160 × 25 × 8.6	309	Dumb Barge	26/08/1938
276	-	160 × 25 × 8.6	309	Dumb Barge	1938
277	-	160 × 25 × 8.6	309	Dumb Barge	1938
278	-	160 × 25 × 8.6	309	Dumb Barge	1939
279	-	160 × 25 × 8.6	309	Dumb Barge	1939
280	-	160 × 25 × 8.6	309	Dumb Barge	1939
281	-	160 × 25 × 8.6	309	Dumb Barge	1939
282	-	160 × 25 × 8.6	309	Dumb Barge	1939
283	-	160 × 25 × 8.6	309	Dumb Barge	1939
284	KHAMIR	160 × 25 × 8.6	309	Dumb Barge	1939
285	KAVAR	160 × 25 × 8.6	309	Dumb Barge	1939
286	KNUNSAR	160 × 25 × 8.6	309	Dumb Barge	1939
287	KHUMAIN	160 × 25 × 8.6	309	Dumb Barge	1939
288	KHARGUN	160 × 25 × 8.6	309	Dumb Barge	1939
289	MSC BISON	86 × 23 × 12	144	Steam Screw Tug	08/03/1939
290	MSC BADGER	86 × 23 × 12	144	Steam Screw Tug	21/04/1939
291	UNDERWOOD	255 × 45 × 21.6	1990	T.S. Motor Cargo Vessel	15/01/1941
292	ORIOLE	160 × 27 × 14	489	S.S. Motor Cargo Vessel	15/08/1939
293	EDINA	160 × 27 × 14	489	S.S. Motor Cargo Vessel	16/10/1939
294	MSC MALLARD	86 × 23 × 12	131	T.S. Diesel Tug	12/12/1939
295	MSC MERLIN		131		
296	-	163 × 28 × 14	500	unknown	1939
297	-	30 × 14 × 7.6	25	Unattended Lightship	11/10/1939
298	-	30 × 14 × 7.6	25	Unattended Lightship	11/10/1939
299	HMS HAZEL	150 × 27.6 × 14.6	463	Tree Class Armed Trawler	27/12/1939

Ship No	Name	Dimensions	Tonnage	Type	Launched
300	HMS *HICKORY*	150 × 27.6 × 14.6	463	Tree Class Armed Trawler	24/02/1940
301	Cancelled			Motor Coaster (Cancelled Order)	
302	Cancelled			Motor Coaster (Cancelled Order)	
303	Cancelled			Motor Coaster (Cancelled Order)	
304	Cancelled			Motor Coaster (Cancelled Order)	
305	Cancelled			Grab Hopper Dredger	

Note: For the list of ships built during the war years, 1939–1945, please refer to the forthcoming *Leith Shipyards at War*, by the same author.

Ship No	Name	Dimensions	Tonnage	Type	Launched
351	*CORNCRAKE*	180 × 32.10 × 20.5	629	S.S. Diesel Cargo	20/12/1945
352	*REDSTART*	180 × 32.10 × 20.5	629	S.S. Diesel Cargo	05/03/1946
353	*KANNA*	210 × 36.6 × 21.8	925	S.S. Diesel Cargo	23/10/1945
354	*KATUI*	210 × 36.6 × 21.8	925	S.S. Diesel Cargo	21/11/1945
355	*TINTO*	280 × 42 × 25.3	1795	S.S. Cargo Steamer	27/08/1946
356	*TRURO*	280 × 42 × 25.3	1795	S.S. Cargo Steamer	11/11/1946
357	*BRAVO*	280 × 42 × 25.3	1798	S.S. Cargo Steamer	06/02/1947
358	*SILVIO*	280 × 42 × 25.3	1798	S.S. Cargo Steamer	18/07/1947
359	*DARINIAN*	255 × 42 × 25	1533	T.S. Diesel Cargo	21/05/1947
360	*PALMELIAN*	255 × 42 × 25	1533	T.S. Diesel Cargo	12/11/1947
361	*KAITANGATA*	290 × 43 × 19.6	2485	T.S. Diesel Cargo	27/01/1948

Ship No	Name	Dimensions	Tonnage	Type	Launched
362	*KONUI*	290 × 43 × 19.6	2485	T.S. Diesel Cargo	25/05/1948
363	*PURIRI*	200 × 39 × 13	1248	T.S. Diesel Cargo	
364	-	80 × 19 × 5.3	85	Barge	
365	-	80 × 19 × 5.3	85	Barge	
366	-	80 × 19 × 5.3	85	Barge	
367	-	80 × 19 × 5.3	85	Barge	
368	-	80 × 19 × 5.3	85	Barge	
369	-	80 × 19 × 5.3	85	Barge	
370	MSC *ONSET*	88 × 24 × 12	154	T.S. Diesel Tug	19/08/1947
371	MSC *ONWARD*	88 × 24 × 12	154	T.S. Diesel Tug	02/09/1947
372	-	50 × 12 × 4.6	150	S.S. Grab Dredger	
373	-	50 × 12 × 4.6	150	S.S. Grab Dredger	
374	*GREBE*	220 × 37 × 21.6	933	S.S. Diesel Cargo	25/03/1948
375	*KAITAWA*	290 × 43 × 19.6	2485	T.S. Diesel Cargo	19/10/1948
376	*KAIAPOI*	290 × 43 × 19.6	2485	T.S. Diesel Cargo	16/03/1949
377	*KAMONA*	235 × 45 × 16	1785	S.S. Diesel Cargo	12/05/1949
378	MSC *GRAB HOPPER No 1*	142 × 30.6 × 13	479	S.S. Diesel Dredger	12/01/1949
379	*MOMBASA*	250 × 43 × 19	2213	T.S. Passenger & Cargo	29/02/1950
380	*MOLE*	130 × 28 × 10.6	311	T.S. Steam Grab Hopper Dredger	15/03/1949
381	MSC *PANTHER*	88 × 24 × 12	154	T.S. Diesel Tug	11/02/1950
382	MSC *PUMA*	88 × 24 × 12	154	T.S. Diesel Tug	17/02/1950
383	-	75 × 20 × 9.6	105	Barge	
384	-	75 × 20 × 9.6	105	Barge	
385	-	75 × 20 × 9.6	105	Barge	
386	-	75 × 20 × 9.6	105	Barge	
387	-	75 × 20 × 9.6	105	Barge	
388	-	75 × 18 × 7.6	103	Water Carrying Barge	
389	*MAMAKU*	175 × 36 × 12.9	927	T.S. Diesel Cargo	28/07/1949
390	-				

Ship No	Name	Dimensions	Tonnage	Type	Launched
391	*KETAM*	95 × 25 × 7.6	125	Hopper Grab Dredger	21/06/1949
392	*CLAROBEN*	81.8 × 20 × 9.6	129	Crude Oil Carrying barge	
393	*MTWARA*	280 × 46 × 27.6	2629	T.S. Passenger & Cargo	20/08/1950
394	*JEAN INGELOW*	99 × 25 × 7.6	149	S.S. Diesel Grab Hopper Dredger	24/03/1950
395	*WANGANUI*	107.6 × 27 × 10.6	252	S.S. Diesel Grab Hopper Dredger	18/01/1950
396	*HIRONDELLE*	196 × 35.6 × 20.4	757	S.S. Diesel Cargo	22/06/1950
397	*SWIFT*	196 × 35.6 × 20.4	757	S.S. Diesel Cargo	19/10/1950
398	*WAIMATE*	325 × 50 × 33.9	3506	S.S. Diesel Cargo	24/06/1951
399	*KAWATIRI*	290 × 43 × 19.6	2484	T.S. Diesel Cargo	06/10/1950
400	*KOKIRI*	290 × 43 × 19.6	2470	T.S. Diesel Cargo	08/09/1951
401	-	57.6 × 8 × 6.6	60	Hopper Barge	
402	-	55 × 17 × 6.6	50	Sugar Barge	
403	-	55 × 17 × 6.6	50	Sugar Barge	
404	-	55 × 17 × 6.6	50	Sugar Barge	
405	-	55 × 17 × 6.6	50	Sugar Barge	
406	*CAVALLO*	290 × 48.6 × 28.3	2340	S.S. Diesel Cargo & Passenger	17/11/1951
407	*TRENTINO*	290 × 48.6 × 28.3	2340	S.S. Diesel Cargo & Passenger	09/04/1952
408	-	43.10 × 25 × 6	35	Dredging Pontoon	
409	-	45.6 × 17.6 × 6.6	45	Hopper Barge	
410	-	45.6 × 17.6 × 6.6	45	Hopper Barge	
411	-	53 × 16.4 × 5	50	Irrigation Barge	
412	MT *HEWITT*	86 × 23 × 12	137	T.S. Diesel Tug	24/04/1951
413	MSC *QUARRY*	88 × 24 × 12	154	T.S. Diesel Tug	01/12/1951
414	MSC *QUEST*	88 × 24 × 12	154	T.S. Diesel Tug	04/11/1952
415	MSC *RANGER*	88 × 24 × 12	154	T.S. Diesel Tug	29/01/1952
416	MSC *ROVER*	88 × 24 × 12	154	T.S. Diesel Tug	17/02/1953
417	*ARUSHA*	112.6 × 32 × 15.3	346	S.S. Steam Tug	17/08/1951
418	*WAREATEA*	240 × 37 × 20	1430	S.S. Diesel Cargo	09/05/1952

Ship No	Name	Dimensions	Tonnage	Type	Launched
419	-	75 × 20 × 9.6	85	Cargo Lighter	
420	-	75 × 20 × 9.6	85	Cargo Lighter	
421	-	75 × 20 × 9.6	85	Cargo Lighter	
422	MT *FOURAH*	110 × 30 × 14.6	306	T.S. Diesel Tug	01/09/1953
423	MT *FARREN*	110 × 30 × 14.6	306	T.S. Diesel Tug	10/06/1952
424	-	40.2 × 26 × 5.11	15	Crane Pontoon	1952
425	-	21 × 15 × 4.3	-	Pontoon	2/12/52
426	*KARUMA*	250 × 41.6 × 25.3	1952	Diesel Cargo	4/01/52
427	*MARWICK HEAD*	250 × 40 × 22.6	1786	Diesel Cargo	1952
428	*LONGFELLOW*	335 × 50 × 26.6		Diesel Cargo	14/04/53
429	*DUNNET HEAD*	180 × 31 × 15	748	Diesel Cargo	18/06/53
430	*GOLDEN BAY*	230 × 42 × 18	1659	T.S. Diesel Cement Cargo	27/08/53
431	-	50 × 12 × 4.6		Grab Hopper Dredger (Riveted)	1952
432	-	50 × 12 × 4.6		Grab Hopper Dredger (Welded)	1952
433	-	50 × 12 × 4.6		Grab Hopper Dredger (Welded)	1952
434	*AUBY*	212 × 44 × 21	1733	T.S. Diesel Cargo & Passenger	24/09/1953
435	-	87 × 17.6 × 4.1	100	Barge	
436	-	87 × 17.6 × 4.1	100	Barge	
437	SS *CICERO*	290 × 48.6 × 27	2499	Steamer Cargo/ Passenger	30/06/1954
438	SS *ROLLO*	290 × 48.6 × 27	2499	Steamer Cargo/ Passenger	12/10/1954
439	SS *TEANO*	260 × 43 × 24	1580	Steamer Cargo/ Passenger	23/02/1955
440	MV *ZEALAND*	270 × 45 × 25.6	2030	Diesel Cargo & Passenger	11/11/1954
441	*SAMUEL ARMSTRONG*	128 × 28.6 × 12.6	364	Diesel Grab Dredger	08/03/1956

Ship No	Name	Dimensions	Tonnage	Type	Launched
442	MV *NAVUA*	250 × 41.6 × 25.3	1952	S.S. Diesel Cargo	27/05/1955
443	TSMV *KAITOA*	290 × 43 × 27	2583	T.S. Diesel Cargo	10/05/1956
444	*JOHN HERBERT*	86 × 23 × 12	146	T.S. Diesel Tug	22/06/1955
445	MV *FLAMINIAN*	325 × 50 × 33.9	3100	S.S. Diesel Cargo	09/02/1956
446	*FRANK JAMIESON*	86 × 23 × 12	146	T.S. Diesel Tug	10/08/1956
447	*GANNET*	95 × 25 × 7.6	250	Diesel Grab Dredger	02/12/1953
448	MV *KAIMAI*	250 × 41.6 × 25.3	2007	S.S. Diesel Cargo	08/06/1956
449	MV *TENNYSON*	335 × 50 × 26.6	3894	S.S. Diesel Cargo	20/11/1956
450	*LAKE LOTHING*	156 × 34 × 17	659	Diesel Grab Dredger	05/04/1955
451	-	75 × 20 × 9.6	105	Barge	
452	-	75 × 20 × 9.6	105	Barge	
453	-	75 × 20 × 9.6	105	Barge	
454	-	75 × 20 × 9.6	105	Barge	
455	*ANNAHDA*	110 × 29 × 10.6	281	S.S. Diesel Grab Dredger	27/03/1956
456	MV *KUMALLA*	235 × 45 × 15.3	1946	S.S. Diesel Cargo	09/11/1956
457	MV *KONINI*	250 × 41.6 × 25.3	2007	S.S. Diesel Cargo	15/02/1957
458	MV *SANDPIPER*	215 × 36.6 × 20.6	916	S.S. Diesel Cargo	01/05/1957
459	MV *THACKERAY*	345 × 54 × 29	4650	S.S. Diesel Cargo	12/02/1958
460	HMS *TYPHOON*	180 × 38.6 × 18	1034	S.S. Diesel Ocean Salvage Tug	14/10/1958
461	MV *KOONYA*	235 × 45 × 15.3	1946	S.S. Diesel Cargo	16/10/1957
462	MV *MALATIAN*	250 × 42.6 × 15	1420	S.S. Diesel Cargo	17/04/1958
463	MV *CATANIAN*	250 × 42.6 × 15	1420	S.S. Diesel Cargo	28/08/1958
464	MV *PATEENA*	250 × 43 × 17.6	2200	S.S. Diesel Cargo	07/11/1958
465	MV *POOLTA*	250 × 43 × 17.6	2200	S.S. Diesel Cargo	13/05/1959
466	-		80	Dredging Pontoon	
467	*CRAIGLEITH*	88 × 25 × 12.6	175	S.S. Diesel Tug	16/05/1958
468	MV *MACAULAY*	345 × 54 × 29	4650	S.S. Diesel Cargo	11/12/1958
469	-			Ramp Ended Pontoon	
470	*MARABOU*	130 × 30.6 × 9	310	T.S. Grab Dredger	13/02/1959

Ship No	Name	Dimensions	Tonnage	Type	Launched
471	MV *AARO*	300 × 48.6 × 19.9	2600	S.S. Diesel Cargo	19/08/1959
472	MV *RAPALLO*	340 × 54 × 31	3400	S.S. Diesel Cargo	26/04/1960
473	MV *ARCADIAN*	340 × 54 × 31	3400	S.S. Diesel Cargo	27/07/1960
474	*CRESWELL*	128.6 × 28.6 × 12	374	S.S. Grab Dredger	16/06/1959
475	*CHARLES HEARN*	86 × 23 × 12	139	T.S. Diesel Tug	16/09/1959
476	*COSRAY 23*	185 × 50 × 8	573	Rock Barge (Tipping)	15/04/1960
477	*COSRAY 24*	185 × 50 × 8	573	Rock Barge (Tipping)	28/04/1960
478	*JOHN WILSON*	246 × 42 × 18.6	1675	Bulk Cement Carrier	15/04/1961
479	LDC *No 5*	90 × 15.6 × 6	100	Rock Barge (Tipping)	16/01/1961
480	LDC *No 6*	90 × 15.6 × 6	100	Rock Barge (Tipping)	03/03/1961
481	*TORO*	162.6 × 33 × 10.6	512	River & Esty Tanker	09/10/1961
482	RFA *HEBE*	350 × 55 × 31	4823	S.S. Diesel Cargo	18/06/1962
483	RFA *BACCHUS*	350 × 55 × 31	4823	S.S. Diesel Cargo	16/11/1962
484	*UNO*	162.6 × 33 × 10.6	530	River & Esty Tanker	14/12/1962
485	*GRAB DREDGER No 1*	210 × 45 × 17.9	1309	Grab Dredger	13/12/1963
486	*HAMBLE*	202 × 36.11 × 15.6	1182	Coastal Tanker	29/04/1964
487	*KILLINGHOLME*	202 × 36.11 × 15.6	1182	Coastal Tanker	30/07/1964
488	*LIGAR BAY*	210 × 38 × 16	1330	Bulk Cement Carrier	10/10/1964
489	LDC *No 7*	90 × 18.10 × 17.10	80	Dumping barge	11/05/1964
490	LDC *No 8*	90 × 18.10 × 17.10	80	Dumping barge	07/12/1964
491	*ABDUL MALIKI*	85 × 24.3 × 12	154	T.S. Diesel Tug	04/02/1965
492	*ASTRO*	167.6 × 33 × 11.6	550	River & Esty Tanker	28/11/1964
493	*TRIBENI*	175 × 35 × 17	918	T.S. Survey Vessel	30/06/1965
494	*GEORGE OHIKERE*	85 × 24.3 × 12	154	T.S. Diesel Tug	19/03/1965
495	*SALERNO*	280 × 45.6 × 26	1559	S.S. Diesel Cargo	24/11/1965

Ship No	Name	Dimensions	Tonnage	Type	Launched
496	*SALMO*	280 × 45.6 × 26	1559	S.S. Diesel Cargo	12/12/1966
497	*SORRENTO*	280 × 45.6 × 26	1559	S.S. Diesel Cargo	24/05/1967
498	*SILVIO*	280 × 45.6 × 26	1559	S.S. Diesel Cargo	30/11/1967
499	*SANGRO*	280 × 45.6 × 26	1523	S.S. Diesel Cargo	14/03/1968
500	RFA *ENGADINE*	385 × 58 × 35.4	6384	Helicopter Support Ship	16/09/1966
501	*ATHENIAN*	280 × 45.6 × 26	1587	S.S. Diesel Cargo	04/05/1966
502	*ARO*	125 × 28.6 × 11.6	339	Grab Dredger	10/10/1967
503	*MEDITERRANEAN*	280 × 47.6 × 26	1459	S.S. Diesel Cargo	20/10/1968
504	*EIGAMOIYA*	335 × 58 × 15.3	4426	S.S. Diesel Cargo	19/04/1969
505	*HEDWIN*	146.6 × 39 × 12 ft	666	Grab Hopper Dredger	20/03/1969
506	*PORT TUDY*	94 × 15.6 × 8 m	3060	S.S. Motor Tanker	13/09/1969
507	*SPEEDWAY*	81 × 16.5 × 4m	1160	S.S. Vehicle Transporter	18/02/1970
508	RRS *BRANSFIELD*	90 × 18.3 × 9.5 m	4816	S.S. Antarctic Survey Vessel	04/09/1970
509	*LLOYDSMAN*	67.21 × 14.172 × 8.5	2041	Ocean Salvage Tug	17/02/1971
510	*CARIBBEAN PROGRESS*	104 × 20.3 × 12.5 m	3822	T.S. Ro/Ro Container Ship	05/10/1971
511	*HERO*	105 × 19 × 12 m	3468	Ro/Ro Trailer Transport	28/12/1972
512	HMS *HERALD*	235 × 49 × 25.9 ft	2533	Ocean Survey Vessel	04/10/1973
513	RMAS *GOOSANDER*	48.8 × 12.2 × 5.5 ft	923	Boom Defence Vessel	12/04/1973
514	RMAS *POCHARD*	48.8 × 12.2 × 5.5 ft	923	Boom Defence Vessel	07/12/1973
515	*PIONEER*	61 × 13.42 × 4 m	1071	Passenger Vehicle Ferry	01/04/1974
516	*S A WOLRAAD WOLTEMADE*	85 × 15.2 × 8.6 m	2822	Ocean Salvage Tug	23/04/1976
517	*DUCHRAY*	34 × 9.2 × 4.5 m	330	Harbour Tug	27/06/1975

Ship No	Name	Dimensions	Tonnage	Type	Launched
518	*BOQUHAN*	34 × 9.2 × 4.5 m	326	Harbour Tug	14/08/1975
519	*FLYING CHILDERS*	34 × 9.2 × 4.5 m	326	Harbour Tug	18/12/1975
520	*GARRISON POINT*	120 × 19.5 × 11.5 m	7702	Bulk Carrier	05/08/1976
521	*BORTHWICK*	73.2 × 12.8 × 6 m	1569	Gas Tanker	23/03/1977
522	*CLAYMORE*	70 × 15.5 × 4.8 m	1871	Passenger Vehicle Ferry	28/12/1978
523	*RHINO*	66 × 13.4 × 6.5 m	1445	Mini Bulk Carrier	10/04/1978
524	*DP-ZPS-6*	36.6 × 18.5 × 3.66	290	Crane Barge	27/02/1979
525	*DP-ZPS-7*	36.6 × 18.5 × 3.66	290	Crane Barge	10/05/1979
526	*BAJIMA*	34 × 9.2 × 4.5 m	326	T.S. Diesel Tug	28/03/1980
527	*BURUTU*	34 × 9.2 × 4.5 m	326	T.S. Diesel Tug	15/05/1980
528	-	33 × 23 × 1.5	-	MacBridge Unit	
529	*MERSEY MARINER*	73.5 × 15.5 × 6.25 m	2191	Grab Hopper Dredger	04/02/1981
530	THV *PATRICIA*	77.8 × 13.8 × 6.9 m	2639	Light house Supply Ship	30/09/1981
531	*SEAFORTH SOVEREIGN*	55.2 × 13.15 × 6.15 m	1199	Offshore Supply Ship	20/05/1982
532	*BALDER LEITH*	56.4 × 13.8 × 6.9 m	1032	Offshore Supply Ship	18/01/1983
533	-	16.72 × 17 × 7.4 m	30	Experimental Submarine Test Vessel	-
534	*ST CATHERINE*	75 × 16.8 × 4.5 m	2036	Passenger/car ferry	30/03/1983
535	*ST HELEN*	75 × 16.8 × 4.5 m	2983	Passenger/car ferry	15/09/1983

ST Helen launched and little did we know she would be the last ship launched at Leith

GLOSSARY

Shipbuilding has developed its own language, with thousands of words coined over time to explain the particulars of working on the build of a vessel or when working on it. Some are only used in boatbuilding and some are specific to steel shipbuilding, while others can relate to either segment of what is a vast and complex industry.

Shipbuilding and nautical terms

ABV	*armed boarding vessel*
Anchor	A heavy, pick-like device attached to a boat's stem by a **warp** and chain. Modern anchors are made of steel; common types of anchor are plough, fisherman and Danforth. The chain, which connects the anchor to its warp, is fixed onto the lower anchor end, adding weight and preventing chafing of the warp on rocks or shellfish beds.
Aft peak	Compartment in the after end of the stern, aft of the aft peak watertight bulkhead or after collision bulkhead.
Amidships	At or near the mid-ship section of the ship.
Angle iron	Name given to the steel or iron section used in the ships construction, can have equal flange length or with one flange longer than the other used to rivet through to the shell plating.
AP (After perpendicular)	A line vertical from the baseline, usually taken from the after side of the rudder stock, or sometimes through the centre of the rudder stock. This line is taken up to where it intersects with the **load** or reference **waterline**. From the point where that load waterline passes through the ship's stem is created the FP or Forward Perpendicular. The distance between the two lines, known as length between perpendiculars or LBP, is divided up by the naval architect to create what is known as frame stations. They will form the grid whereby the naval architect will begin to create the small-scale lines for the ship known as scantling lines. (see also under **loftsman**).
Athwartship	Deck beams are laid athwartship; that is, across the vessel, at right angles to the ship's centre line.
Ballast	Used to trim the vessel, can be sea water moved from tank to tank or weight in the form of pig Iron or concrete to help with the ship's stability.
Base line	The design line that all forward and aft measurements are taken from: the **AP** or the **FP**. All height measurements are taken from the baseline; in the case of a **drop keel** these heights will be shown as a minus. These measurements are used to create part of the **offset table**.
Battens	Long strips of wood used in the Loft for fairing lines, also used as protective strips in cargo holds.
Beam	The maximum width of the ship.

Beam knee	A bracket holding the transverse deck beam to the vertical frames at the side of the hull.
Bevel	The angle between two plates or flanges when greater than a right angle it is said to be an open bevel, or when less it is a closed bevel. Can also be used to describe a chamfer.
Bilge	The lowest part of the hull interior, under the **sole**. Water and or fuel tanks are often placed in the bilges to lower the centre of gravity and so help keep the ship upright.
Bilge blocks	Wooden blocks placed under the **bilge** to support during construction or for when the ship goes into dry dock.
Bilge keel	A longitudinal, external, underwater member used to reduce a ship's tendency to roll and to aid directional stability. In Britain twin bilge keels are often used on small boats moored in estuaries with a large tidal range so the boat stays upright when the mooring dries out. With their much shallower draft, yachts of this type can be sailed in shallow waters. Not as hydrodynamically efficient as a fin keel. Designed to break if a ship hits an underwater obstacle, thus helping to protect the **shell** or **bilge strake**.
Bilge pump	A pump, either manual or electric, with the inlet set at the lowest point in the bilges, where water will collect when the boat is upright. The inlet is protected by a screen to stop blockages.
Bilge strake	The strake of plate that forms the bilge.
Binnacle	A stand or box where the ship's compass, adjusting magnets and lamp are kept, this can all be in a box on a small boat or yacht.
Bitt	A vertical steel pillar used to make fast lines, also sometimes referred to as bollards when two posts are used.
Bitter end	The bit found in the chain locker where the anchor chain is attached. You do not wish the chain to reach this point, hence the old saying 'to the bitter end'.
Black Squad	The collective name for all the steelworking trades that built a ship.
Block	See **pulley**.
Boat deck	As the name implies, a deck where working boats or lifeboats are stowed.
Body plan	The drawing that shows the ship's frame lines either full size or to scale. This is a view looking on the bow of the ship, and when full size the after portion of the ship is superimposed on top to save space on the loft floor.
Boss	The curved plate surrounding the outboard swelling of the shaft.
Boss plate	A curved shell plate covering the **boss**; this can be a complex shape with double curvature.
Bow	The front, and generally sharp, end of the hull. It is designed to reduce the resistance of the hull cutting through water, and should be tall enough to prevent water from easily washing over the deck of the hull. The bulbous bow designed into some larger ships since the 1920s improves speed and stability.
Bowsprit	On a sailing ship, a spar that extends forward from the foredeck, outboard of the hull proper. They were common in square-rigged ships, where they were used to attach the outer or flying jib. In modern sailing boats they are often made of lightweight carbon and are used to attach the **luff** of lightweight sails such as spinnakers.
Breakwater	A plate erected on the foc'sle deck arranged in a V shape to spread/prevent solid water sweeping the decks in heavy seas.
Breast hook	The brackets that hold the shape of the **soft nose**.
Bridge	(*in shipbuilding*) A means of temporarily connecting two plates together to be **faired** and welded. Also the name given to the upper area of the ship where the wheelhouse is situated.
Bulkhead	The internal transverse structure of the hull; the number of bulkheads is determined by the length of the ship under class rules.
Bulwark	The upstanding part of the topsides around the edges of the deck, providing some security when a boat is heeled.

Butt	The joint formed when two plates are put edge to edge. Vertical joints on a ship are known as butts, while horizontal joints are known as seams.
Butt strap	A plate used to connect, by riveting, two plates placed edge to edge, to give a smooth or fair outer surface.
Buttock	A profile cut at a given distance from the centre line of the ship, this will show as a curved line in the ships profile or sheer view, shown on the lines plan drawings as one of the three primary views.
Buttock lines	The intersection of the moulded surface with a vertical plane at any given distance from the centreline of the ship
Camber	The curvature of the deck transversely or athwartships the difference in height between the centre of the deck and the deck at side.
Cant frame	A frame that is not at right angles to the ships centre line, usually found at the stern of a cruiser/counter or round type stern. The beams fan out from the after peak bulkhead to help support the deck.
Capstan	A vertical metal or wooden winch secured to the foredeck of a ship, used for hoisting the anchor. Capstans may be manually operated, or powered hydraulically or electrically. A traditional sailor-powered wooden capstan is fitted with removable spoke-like wooden arms which the sailors push round and round, often in time to a sea shanty or chant.
Caulking	Making a joint watertight.
Chart room	A small room usually just aft of the bridge, where navigation is carried out using the available and up-to-date charts.
Coaming	The vertical side plate of a hatch or skylight
Cofferdam	A watertight space between two plates or bulkheads.
Coffin plate	The plate joining two side plates over the **keel** of a vessel at the **stern,** which in plan **view** creates a shape similar to a coffin lid.
Collision bulkhead	The most forward watertight bulkhead close to the bow, this bulkhead is positioned according to Lloyd's rules for shipbuilding.
Complement	The full number of people required to operate a ship. Includes officers and crew members; does not include passengers. The number of people assigned to a warship in peacetime may be considerably less than her full complement.
Counter stern	A traditional stern construction with a long overhang and a shorter, upright, end piece. The counter is usually decked over. The stern is rounded when seen in plan **view**. Other shapes of stern are **transom**, elliptical and round.
Countersink	To taper a hole for a flush rivet or bolt.
Cube	The cargo-carrying capacity of a ship, measured in cubic feet. There are two common types:
	Bale Cube (or *Bale Capacity*) A measurement of capacity for cargo in bales, on pallets etc., where the cargo does not conform to the shape of the ship. The space available for cargo is measured in cubic feet to the inside of the cargo battens on the frames, and to the underside of the beams.
	Grain Cube (or *Grain Capacity*) A measurement of capacity for cargo like grain, which flows to conform to the shape of the ship. The maximum space available for cargo is measured in cubic feet, the measurement being taken to the inside of the shell plating of the ship or to the outside of the frames, and to the top of the beam or underside of the deck plating.
Deadrise	The rise of bottom. It is the difference in height between the **base line** and the point where the straight line through the flat of bottom surface would intersect the Flat of Side of the **moulded surface** at its widest point.
Deck	The top surface of the hull, which keeps water and weather out of the hull, and allows the crew, standing and walking on it, to operate the boat more easily. It stiffens the hull. Temporary frames (or moulds) can be removed and kept for building another boat.

Displacement		A measurement of the weight of the vessel, usually used for warships. (Merchant ships are usually measured based on the volume of cargo space; see **Tonnage.**) Displacement is expressed either in long tons of 2,240 lbs, or in metric tonnes of 1,000 kg. Since the two units are very close in size (2,240 pounds = 1,016 kg and 1,000 kg = 2,205 lbs), it is common not to distinguish between them. To preserve secrecy, nations sometimes mis-state a warship's displacement.
	Displacement, light	The weight of the ship excluding cargo, fuel, ballast, stores, passengers and crew, but with water in the boilers to steaming level.
	Displacement, loaded	The weight of the ship, including cargo, passengers, fuel, water, stores, dunnage and other items necessary for use on a voyage, which brings the vessel down to her load draft.
	Deadweight tons (DWT)	A measure of the ship's total carrying capacity. It's the difference between **displacement, light** and **displacement, loaded**.
	Cargo deadweight tons	The weight remaining after deducting fuel, water, stores, dunnage and other items necessary for use on a voyage, from the deadweight of the vessel.
Dog		A means of holding down iron or steel plate. The more dogs required for a plate the more distortion found in it; this is usually due to poor welding sequence, and a sign of re-work needed, hence many more man-hours to do a job that has not been dimensionally controlled.
Double bottom		Forms a watertight barrier on the bottom of the ship, extending from the keel to the tank top. It is used to store ballast water, and creates another layer of protection should the ship be holed below the tank top.
Draught		Distance from the bottom of the keel to the **waterline**. It may be spelt 'draft'.
Draught, loaded		The depth of water necessary to float a vessel fully loaded.
Drop keel		A retractable or removable fin / centreboard / daggerboard.
Fairing		(*in shipbuilding*) ensuring that material put in place is correctly located
Forward perpendicular (FP)		See **AP, After perpendicular**.
Frame		The transverse structure that gives a boat its cross-sectional shape. Frames may be solid or peripheral. They may be made of wood, plywood, steel, aluminium or composite materials. They may be removed after construction to save weight, or be reused, or left *in situ*, as in wooden boatbuilding. In ancient shipbuilding the frames were put in after the planking, but now most boats are built with the frames first. This gives greater control over the shape. In old, heavily built square-rigged ships, the frames were made up of four individual timbers – futtocks – as it was impossible to make the shape from a single piece of wood. The futtock closest to the keel was the ground futtock and the other pieces were called upper futtocks.
Frame lines		The transverse intersections of the **moulded surface/line** with a vertical plane cut transverse across the vessel. Frame Lines are curved in the Body **view**, showing the shape of the vessel, while in the Half-breadth view or the Profile view they are shown as straight lines.
Freeboard		The distance between the **waterline** and the **deck** when the vessel is loaded. Boats using sheltered waters can have low freeboard, but seagoing vessels need high freeboard.
Freeboard, moulded		The difference between the moulded depth and the moulded draft. (It is the height of the side of the vessel which is above the water when she floats at her **load waterline**.)
Graving dock		Dry dock.
Gunwale		The upper, outside longitudinal structural member of the **hull**.
Hatch		A lifting or sliding opening into a cabin, or through the deck for loading and unloading cargo.

Heads	Marine toilet. An abbreviation of the term 'catheads', which, up at the bow, were the normal place for toileting in square-rigger days. Always used in the plural. (The designed function of the catheads, timbers set outboard of the hull, was to provide protection for the hull against the friction of the anchor warp.)
Howff	The inner sanctum within some shipyards, usually trade-specific, so the shipwrights in their various groups would have howffs scattered around the shipyard: the platers would have their own howff, as would the welders, and so on.
Hull	The main body of a ship or boat, including her bottom, sides and deck. Some people are surprised to find that in a modern ship of any size the hull, for most of its length, has a flat bottom the full width of the ship. This is, however, essential for stability, because when such a ship heels then on its lower side there is a greater air-filled volume under the water than on the upper side, thus pushing the ship back upright, countering the heel.
Iron fighters	A colloquial west of Scotland / Clyde shipbuilding term for the **Black Squad**.
Keel	The main central member along the length of the bottom of the ship or boat. It is an important part of the ship's structure, with a strong influence on its turning performance, and in sailing ships the keel resists the sideways pressure of the wind, enabling the course to be steered.
Keelson	An internal beam fixed to the top of the **keel** to strengthen the joint of the upper members of the ship to the keel.
Kevlar	A hi-tech and very strong synthetic material, used for cables, bulletproof jackets etc, developed by DuPont in the 1960s.
Knuckle	Where a plate changes angle or direction (effectively creates a fold in a plate); a good way of reducing the amount of welding required. This method of platework also reduces distortion when carried out properly.
Length	The distance between the forwardmost and aftermost parts of the ship.
	Length overall (LOA) — The maximum length of the ship.
	Length when submerged (LOS) — The maximum length of the submerged hull measured parallel to the designed **load waterline**.
	Length at waterline (LWL) — The ship's length measured at the **waterline**.
Lines drawing	A plan showing the three principal **views**: sheer or profile view, half-breadth or plan view, and body view. The lines drawing is the 2D representation of the 3D moulded surface of the vessel.
Load waterline	A line created during the initial design phase of a ship; it starts as a reference waterline showing where the ship can be loaded up to. During the ship's life the load waterline may be changed, but the original design reference waterline will always be so.
Lofting	The process used to create life-size drawings of **frames** so they can be manufactured. Today frames can be cut with extreme accuracy by a robot directly from a computer program.
Loftsman	The loftsman (loft) was responsible for taking the scaled-down naval architect's scantling lines and producing them full size or one-tenth-scale so the ship's form could be made. The loft then took the finished faired offsets from this and developed the **shell** plating and all the other steelwork involved in building the vessel. Templates were made so that the curved forms could be cut out of steel full size, along with the dimensional control of the build. Today this is all done by computer aided design (CAD) generating a 3D model from which the ship's production drawings are taken. The role of the loft has been replaced by the designer and the nesting team, the dimensional control team, and quality control and planning.
Longitudinals	Stiffening members that run fore and aft on a ship. They can be **shell** longitudinals or **deck** longitudinals.
Luff	The front part of a fore-and-aft sail, attached to either the **mast** or a **stay**.

Mast	A vertical pole on a ship which supports sails and/or rigging. If it's a wooden multi-part mast, this term applies specifically to the lowest portion.
Mast step	A socket, often strengthened, to take the downward thrust of the mast and hold its foot in position. In smaller craft, the mast step may be on the keel or on the deck.
Mizzen	In a sailing boat with two or more masts, a permanent mast and sail set aft of the mainmast.
Moulded surface/ moulded line	The inside surface of the plating of a ship. The moulded surface has no thickness and is fair and smooth. Usually, but not always, once the ship is built the plating will extend outside of the moulded surface. The heel of each **shell** frame is on this moulded surface, commonly known as the moulded line, and it is the start point for the design of the vessel, consisting of station lines, frame lines, waterlines and buttocks. The points on these intersections create the moulded surface. It should be remembered that this moulded surface is theoretical and is not an actual part of the ship. It is exactly the shape which an infinitely thin piece of sheet rubber would take if stretched tightly over the shell frames and main deck beams, with no plating in place. (Once I gave this description, using another word for the rubber sheet, in an interview, and they almost fell off their seats.)
Offset table	Used in ship design; contains measurements that give the coordinates for the lines plan (showing the points that form the curved lines that indicate the shape of the hull).
O-Gee	The line of the shaped plate that forms the 3D line from the main deck to the forecastle deck at the ship's side.
Parallel middle body	The straight part at the centre of the ship, also known as the Flat of Side, and common in large slab-sided vessels. Not something that any of the Leith-built ships had, as most were complex-shaped ships.
Planing	When the bow of the ship or boat, moving rapidly, lifts clear of the water. This is more hydrodynamically efficient, so is designed into speedy vessels.
Port	The left side of the ship when looking forward; so called by the Vikings as this was the side that would go alongside a harbour wall. The opposite side of the vessel from **starboard**.
Pratique	The licence given to a ship to enter the port on assurance from the captain to the authorities that she is free from contagious disease. The clearance granted is commonly referred to as Free Pratique.
Pulley	A small, part-enclosed wheel used to help redirect the angle of a rope or, in combination with more pulleys set up as a block and tackle, to reduce the power needed to pull the object controlled by the rope.
Rigging (running)	The ropes or cables used in sailing ships to control the sails. Cables are of two types: Type 7 × 7: a semi-flexible wire used for luff wires in sails, halyards (sometimes plastic-coated) trapeze wires and light halyards. Type 7 × 19, which is used for all halyards, wire sheets, vangs and strops that must run through a pulley.
Rigging (standing)	Wires rods, cables or ropes used to keep a mast upright. Since the 1960s stainless steel wire has become universal in the developed world. Elsewhere galvanised wire or even rope may be used because of its availability and cheapness. The type of stainless steel wire commonly used in standing rigging such as stays is Type 1 × 19: a non-flexible wire. The common way of attaching wire is to form a small loop at the end which is fixed in place by clamping a soft metal swag over the free ends. (Talurite is a common brand of swagging.) The wire loop is then fastened to a rigging screw, with a bow shackle to the chain plate. In small sailing boats Kevlar rope is sometimes used in place of wire.
Scuppers	Gaps in the bulwarks which enable seawater or rainwater to flow off the deck.
Shackle	A quick-release metal device used to connect cables to fixings.

Shaft horsepower (SHP)	The amount of mechanical power delivered by the engine to a propeller shaft. In the SI system of units one horsepower is equivalent to 746 watts.
Sheave	A **pulley**.
Sheer	The generally curved shape of the top of the **hull** when viewed in profile. The sheer is traditionally lowest amidships, to maximise **freeboard** at the ends of the hull. Sheer can also be reverse – higher in the middle to maximise space inside – or straight, or a combination of shapes.
Sheet	A rope used to control the position of a sail, e.g. the main sheet controls the position of the main sail.
Shell	Its principal function is to act as a watertight skin for the vessel. Also known as the **hull**.
Skeg	A long, tapering piece of timber fixed to the underside of a **keel** near the **stern** in a small boat, especially a kayak or rowing boat, to aid directional stability.
Soft nose	The upper strakes of plate that form the bow of the ship, extending from the solid stem bar to the main deck.
Spar	A length of timber, aluminium, steel or carbon fibre of approximately round or pear-shaped section, used to support sails; types of spar include a **mast**, boom, gaff, yard, **bowsprit**, prod, boomkin, pole and dolphin striker.
Spring	The amount of curvature in the keel from **bow** to **stern** when viewed side on. The modern trend is to have less spring (known as hogging or sagging) in order to have less disturbance to water flow at higher speeds, thus aiding **planing**.
Starboard	The right side of the ship when looking forward. The word comes from the Viking, whose ships had a *styrbord*, steering oar, on that side. The opposite side of the vessel from **port**.
Stays	See **rigging (standing)**.
Steamer	Steam-powered cargo or passenger ship.
Stem	A continuation of the **keel** upwards at the front of the **hull**.
Stern	The back of the boat.
Strake	A strip of material running longitudinally along the vessel's side, bilge or bottom. On a steel boat each longitudinal strake of plating has a name, such as Garboard strake, Bilge strake and Sheer strake, with any strakes of plating in between labelled A, B, C etc.
Strong back	A heavy plate used as a **fairing** aid to keep plates straight and fair, and to assist in the alignment before and during welding.
Swag	See **rigging (standing)**.
Taff rail	A railing, often ornate, at the extreme stern of a traditional square-rigged ship. In light air conditions an extra sail would be set on a temporary mast from the taff rail.
Ton	The unit of measure often used in specifying the size of a ship. There are three completely unrelated definitions for the word; two of them refer to volume (the word was originally 'tun', a large barrel) and the third definition relates to weight.
	Measurement ton (M/T) or *Ship ton* — Calculated as 40 cubic feet of cargo space. See **cube: bale cube**. For example, a vessel with a capacity of 10,000 M/T has a bale cubic of 400,000 cubic feet.
	Register ton — A measurement of cargo-carrying capacity in cubic feet. One register ton is equivalent to 100 cubic feet of cargo space.
	Weight ton (W/T) — Calculated as a long ton (2,240 lbs).
Tonnage	A measurement of the cargo-carrying capacity of merchant vessels. It depends not on weight but on the volume available for carrying cargo. The basic units of measure are the Register Ton, equivalent to 100 cubic feet, and the Measurement Ton, equivalent to 40 cubic feet. The calculation of tonnage is complicated by many technical factors.

	Gross tons	The entire internal cubic capacity of the ship expressed in tons of 100 cubic feet to the ton, except certain spaces which are exempted such as: peak and other tanks for water ballast, open forecastle bridge and poop, access of hatchways, certain light and air spaces, domes of skylights, condenser, anchor gear, steering gear, wheelhouse, galley and cabin for passengers.
	Net tons	Obtained from the gross tonnage by deducting crew and navigating spaces and making allowances for propulsion machinery.
Transom		A wide, flat or slightly curved, sometimes vertical, board at the rear of the hull, which on small power boats is often designed to carry an outboard motor. Transoms increase width and buoyancy at the stern. On a boat designed to be powered by an outboard, the stern is often the widest point, to provide displacement to carry the heavy outboard and to resist the initial downward thrust of the craft when it's **planing**.
Views		The three main views of a ship are:
	Body view	The view showing the true shapes of the frame lines. They are curved, while buttocks and waterlines are straight. It is drawn in two parts: the right-hand part is looking directly aft at the port side of the moulded surface, while the other part is looking directly forward at the after half of the port side.
	Profile or sheer view	The view looking at the moulded lines from starboard to port. The curve of the deck, the sheerline (which gives the alternative name to this view), is shown as a nice fair curve, while the waterlines and the frame lines are straight.
	Half-breadth or plan view	The view looking down on the vessel's moulded surface. The waterlines are their true shape, while the frame lines and buttocks are straight. To save space only the port side of the vessel is drawn, the starboard side being symmetrically opposite.
Warp		A rope normally used for holding a vessel in place, either alongside a quay or another vessel, or to a buoy or anchor.
Waterline		The intersections of the **moulded surface** at a given height on a horizontal plane. The 3-metre waterline is a section cut 3 metres above the base horizontal. Waterlines are curved in the half-breadth **view**, straight vertical lines in the body view, and straight horizontal lines in the sheer view.

SOURCES

I have tried to write this book to appeal not only to the ex-shipbuilder or to someone from Leith, but with a much wider range of readers in mind.

The sources used come from a very broad range of information, with some of the best information direct from men and women who were there, not just from dry research in dusty old library archives – although through necessity they become very important, as we are slowly losing a lot of our great maritime history. This book, the fourth in a series of five, is my individual attempt to keep some of that history alive. The ships built during the Second World War will have a book covering that time at the Leith Shipyards, completing the history of the yards.

First-hand comments sent to my original website on the Leith shipyards have been saved where possible, and used in the category where they were originally placed.

I have made much use of the internet; my own original website was a very good source of material, which I have used extensively throughout the series.

Where I have found contradictory sources, I have used my own judgement as a shipbuilder, along with the shipyard's original build order books even though some of the early entries are missing or unclear, to reach a conclusion.

The following are some websites that you may find useful:

www.theloftsman.com

http://www.imo.org

http://www.portgermeinhistory.com/KobenhavnDiaries.html#voyages for the sources, on the voyages that *København* made to Australia.

https://www.nrscotland.gov.uk/record-keeping/national-register-of-archives-for-scotland/search-the-online-register

M/S Maritime Museum of Denmark, Ny Kronborgvej 1, DK-3000 Elsinore. info@mfs.dk +45 49210685 https://mfs.dk/en/knowledge-center/

Scottish newspapers

www.archive.scotsman.com. You will be charged a fee to access its records.

Other Edinburgh newspapers are held on microfilm in the Edinburgh Room, Edinburgh Central Library, King George IV Bridge, Edinburgh, EH1 1 EG. edinburgh.room@edinburgh.gov.uk .

Glasgow newspapers are held by the Mitchell Library, North Street, Glasgow, G3 7DN. archives@cls.glasgow.gov.uk .

I have found that the museums and state libraries of Australia, including those in Adelaide, Victoria, New South Wales and Brisbane, have all been a very helpful resource for information.

Museums in New Zealand have once more been very helpful and a good source of information. It is, though, a little bit surprising that none of the Scottish maritime museums have much if anything on shipbuilding at Leith; perhaps one day Leith may have her own to showcase her rich maritime heritage.

Of course, we should not discount Wikipedia; research just takes a little bit longer, as one does need to check the information shown. But as a starting point, and at no cost, you will not find better.

Finally, if there is a particular ship you are interested in and you have the name and the year built, type those details into an internet search engine, and you should be able to find some information about it.